Monopoly F

Monopoly Politics

James C. Miller III

HOOVER INSTITUTION PRESS

Stanford University   Stanford, California

www-hoover.stanford.edu

Hoover Institution Press Publication No. 457

Copyright © 1999 by the Board of Trustees of the
Leland Stanford Junior University

First printing, 1999

04 03 02 01 00 99   9 8 7 6 5 4 3 2 1

Manufactured in the United States of America

The paper used in this publication meets the minimum requirements
of American National Standard for Information Sciences—Permanence
of Paper for Printed Library Materials, ANSI Z39.48–1984. ⊗

Library of Congress Cataloging-in-Publication Data
Miller, James Clifford.
  Monopoly politics / James C. Miller III.
      p.   cm.
  Includes bibliographical references.
  ISBN 0-8179-9652-4 (alk. paper)
  1. Political science—Economic aspects. 2. Competition.
3. Social choice. I. Title.
JA77.M55   1999
324.7–dc21
                                              99-23021
                                                  CIP

This book is dedicated to my mother,

ANNIE MOSELEY MILLER.

To six children, ten grandchildren, and now one great-grandchild,
she has been a source of pride, hope, help, and inspiration.

CONTENTS

TABLES, FIGURES,
AND CHARTS

PREFACE

This book is an outgrowth of my training as an economist, my work as an antitrust enforcement official, and my experience with politics, politicians, and the electorate.

Economists study how people go about providing for themselves and others—how they earn a living, how they spend their money, and what influences those decisions. Of particular interest to economists is the set of institutions within which people make their economic decisions—property rights, contracts, and the overall organization of production and consumption. It is generally conceded that market-based economies result in higher overall standards of living. For such economies to perform at their peak, however, property rights must be recognized, contracts must be enforced, and, to the degree feasible, production and consumption must be organized *competitively*.

The study of politics is concerned with how people *collectively* make decisions that affect their lives. Seldom do people make these decisions directly but rather through elected representatives of their choosing. How those representatives are selected, how they, in turn, make final determinations, and what effects those decisions have on those they represent would seem to be of significance rivaling the subject matter of conventional economics. After all, by reasonable estimates, economic decisions made collectively, through governments, account for nearly half of the gross domestic product.

After receiving a B.B.A. degree in economics from the University of Georgia in 1964 and commencing work toward a master's in economics, I matriculated in the graduate program at the University of Virginia in 1965. While I was at Virginia, a new subdiscipline of economics and political science, which later became known as "public choice," was under development by a cadre of scholars led by James Buchanan and Gordon Tullock.[1] Their interest was in explaining and assessing the effects of nonmarket decision making using the economist's standard tools of analysis.[2] I learned much from them, but the focus of my study was not public choice, but microeconomics, specifically the organization of production and consumption. In 1969 I received my Ph.D. degree, and over the next decade I taught graduate and undergraduate courses in industrial organization, regulation, and antitrust at a number of universities. I also authored a series of books and articles on these issues.[3]

In 1981, President Ronald Reagan appointed me chairman of the Federal Trade Commission (FTC), one of the agencies with a

1. In 1986, Buchanan was awarded the Nobel Prize for his work in economics and public choice.

2. The original title of the subdiscipline's flagship journal, *Public Choice*, was *Papers in Non-Market Decision Making*.

3. See, for example, *Economic Regulation of Domestic Air Transport: Theory and Policy*, with George W. Douglas (Washington, D.C.: Brookings Institution, 1974); *Perspectives on Federal Transportation Policy* (Washington, D.C.: American Enterprise Institute, 1975); *Benefit-Cost Analysis of Social Regulation: Case Studies from the Council on Wage and Price Stability*, with Bruce Yandle (Washington: American Enterprise Institute, 1979); and *Reforming Regulation*, with Timothy B. Clark and Marvin H. Kosters (Washington, D.C.: American Enterprise Institute, 1980).

responsibility to enforce the federal antitrust laws. (The other is the Antitrust Division of the Department of Justice.) There I was engaged in intensive analysis of the workings of the U.S. economy, the competitiveness of markets, the effectiveness of antitrust enforcement, the performance of the agency that I headed, and reforms I thought would improve the U.S. standard of living. Later, I wrote about these matters in some detail.[4]

Throughout the 1980s, first as FTC chairman and then as President Reagan's budget director (1985–88), I dealt with members of Congress and other elected officials, observing them firsthand—their behavioral patterns and how the various institutions within which they operated (majority voting, the committee system, election versus nonelection years, majority versus nonmajority status, et cetera) affected their overall performance.[5] More important, in 1994, and again in 1996, I became a player in the production side of the political marketplace, offering myself as a candidate for the U.S. Senate. In June 1994, I lost the Republican nomination to represent the state of Virginia in a close convention contest to Colonel Oliver North. In June 1996, I lost a primary contest to Senator John Warner. Both contests gave me valuable insights into the political process—both from the perspective of a candidate and from the perspective of the electorate.

After the loss in 1996, I returned to my academic roots and began to ponder: why are commercial markets organized competitively and perform well, whereas political markets are monopolistic and their performance, while tolerable, is far from

---

4. See *The Federal Trade Commission: The Political Economy of Regulation*, with Robert J. Mackay and Bruce Yandle (Stanford: Hoover Institution Press, 1987) and *The Economist as Reformer: Revamping the FTC, 1981-1985* (Washington, D.C.: American Enterprise Institute, 1989).

5. See *Fix the U.S. Budget: Urgings of an "Abominable No-Man"* (Stanford: Hoover Institution Press, 1994).

ideal? Moreover, I pondered why politicians would be the first to criticize monopoly power in commercial markets but be the last to discover, much less complain about, monopoly power in political markets. Similarly, I pondered why the general public seems to know intuitively that competition is a basic requirement for good performance in commercial markets, is quick to suspect a lack of competitive vigor when problems arise, but seems oblivious to the need for competition in political markets and fails to recognize a lack of competition in such markets (much less demand "demonopolization") as an explanation (or cure) for the poor performance it readily acknowledges.

Musings about these phenomena and discussions with my colleagues at Citizens for a Sound Economy Foundation (CSEF) and at the Center for Study of Public Choice at George Mason University led me to contact the Pew Charitable Trusts, which had just launched a major program of support for work in areas relating to campaign reform. After discussions with Pew vice president Paul Light, there followed a generous grant from the trusts for this project. I am deeply indebted to the trusts, not only for financial support but for encouragement and comments on the work. Among those associated with the trusts, I should mention David B. Magleby, professor and chair of the Department of Political Science at Brigham Young University. Without the support of the Pew Charitable Trusts, my musings would have remained nothing more.

I wish also to thank my colleagues at Citizens for a Sound Economy Foundation and the Tax Foundation. Most especially, I want to thank Parker Normann for extensive research assistance in the preparation of this work. He took a few ideas and little direction and concluded a research agenda that included a thorough and competent summary of the relevant literature. CSEF chairman Boyden Gray, president Paul Beckner, vice president

Matt Kibbe, and director of development Cheryl Hillen offered important support for the effort, as did Patrick Burns, Ty Cobb, Andrew Halataei, Kent Lassman, Scott Moody, Traci Pichler, Jerrie Stewart, and Elizabeth Tobias.

My colleagues in the Center for Study of Public Choice at George Mason gave helpful comments in response to a presentation during December 1997. Remarks by James Buchanan, Roger Congleton, Mark Crain, David Levy, and Robert Tollison were especially helpful, as was research assistance by Jo Anne Burgess. I also profited from rereading Dennis Mueller's excellent survey of work in the field.[6] More than anything else, what differentiates the instant work from others addressing political competition is that it is written from the perspective of a public choice theorist and practitioner. I am lucky to have been a part of this movement almost from the beginning, and I am proud of my association with this body of scholarship.

As usual, my colleagues at the Hoover Institution were extraordinarily helpful and accommodating. Thanks go to Annelise Anderson for her constructive advice on the research, to John Raisian for his support of the project, to Ann Wood for her constructive editing, and to Pat Baker for facilitating the book's publication in a timely manner.

Others contributed by commenting on drafts of this work. Suggestions by Miller Baker, Jack Calfee, Jeff Eisenach, Joe Fogg, John Goolrick, Bill Kovacic, Frank Luntz, Eric O'Keefe, Sam Peltzman, Bob Pitofsky, Larry Sabato, Charles Spies, and Donald Wittman were particularly helpful.

My own family deserves a lot of thanks, especially my wife, Demaris, who holds a Ph.D. in psychology. In June 1998, she

---

6. Dennis C. Mueller, *Public Choice II* (New York: Cambridge University Press, 1989).

won the Republican primary to represent the Eighth District of Virginia in the U.S. Congress—and then lost the November election to incumbent Jim Moran. She's the better politician in the family—and the sparkplug of my life.

Millers' Cabin
Flattop Mountain
Free Union, Virginia
February 1999

"I need [the cabin in order to have] peace and quiet to write a book," said Quinn. "Oh, a writer," said the [real estate] agent, satisfied. "People make allowances for writers as for all other lunatics."

—Frederick Forsyth, *The Negotiator*

CHAPTER ONE

Introduction

Most Americans who live beyond the Washington beltway spend little time thinking about what the federal government is up to. Similarly, except for a few people living in state capitals and those who are employed by state and local governments, few people are preoccupied by state or local politics. America was founded on the notion that government should serve and protect the people, not the other way around. You tend to think more about someone with power over you than someone doing your bidding or just staying out of the way. The extent to which we seemingly neglect or don't think about government is a testament to the success of the American political experiment.

Nevertheless, decisions we make through government can be just as important as those we make in the private sector. Moreover, the *ways* in which we make those decisions matter a lot too, as do the ways in which we make decisions in the commercial world.

PRIVATE VERSUS PUBLIC DECISION MAKING

We make decisions in our social relationships—about our families and our friends, for example—without thinking much about the "exchange" that takes place. "I like you, you like me," is pretty much all there is to it. Whether, and under what circumstances, we have the freedom to make such decisions, of course, depends on government's protecting the liberties we are guaranteed in the Constitution. Freedom to do whatever you want (as long as it's legal) and freedom to associate are important rights of every American. But I want to concentrate on decisions we make through governments that affect us in more material ways and contrast those with decisions we make in the private sector, specifically those we make in commercial markets. (Why I wish to make this contrast will become apparent later.)

In commercial markets, we make decisions *directly*. If we want a new dress, a new computer, and a new car, we may go to Wal-Mart, Computer City, and the Dodge dealer. Or we may go to J.C. Penney's, Radio Shack, and the Toyota dealer. We have a wide range of choice. We make the decisions.

In political markets, we usually make decisions *indirectly*. If we want lower taxes, less spending on defense, and increased Social Security benefits, we choose an *agent* or *representative* to work toward those ends in the political process. Typically, we have a range of choices, including recruiting a candidate to our liking, supporting a candidate with whom we tend to agree, or even becoming a candidate ourselves. But seldom do we have the same degree of direct control as in commercial markets.

WHY PUBLIC DECISIONS ARE IMPORTANT

Decisions we make in commercial markets are extremely important to our well-being. If we pay a lot for a pair of shoes we "just hate," we've made a big mistake. If we purchase a computer with a hard drive that's too small, we won't be able to load all the programs we want to have on hand. If we purchase the wrong car or truck—say it's too small or doesn't get decent gas mileage—we've missed out on something better. Likewise, if we choose the wrong job, or even the wrong profession, our incomes may be lower and job satisfaction may be less than they might have been. In any such case, we've squandered an opportunity. Decisions made in commercial markets are thus important to our material well-being. They can make us happy or they can make us sad, depending on what they are.

Decisions we make through the political process are also important to our material well-being. We don't always get what we want, and the lack of direct control can lead to many frustrations. But overall, the import of the decisions made in political markets rivals in importance those made in commercial markets. The fraction of the total economy that is directed by the decisions we as voters make in political markets is huge. During 1998, the U.S. economy turned out approximately $8.40 trillion in goods and services, or gross domestic product (GDP). Total federal spending during the period was $1.65 trillion, or 19.7 percent of total GDP.[1] Spending by state and local governments during 1998 was another 12.7 percent.[2] Thus, governments spending at all levels accounted for almost one-third of GDP.

This measure both overestimates and underestimates the importance of the economic decisions we make collectively. It overestimates the public sector's importance because much government spending is not for goods and services, but to transfer funds from some individuals to others. For example, Social Security spending is a transfer from those who pay Social Security (FICA) taxes to those who receive Social Security checks. Likewise, Medicare spending is a transfer from those who pay Medicare premiums (plus taxpayers in general) to those who provide services

1. "The Economic and Budget Outlook for Fiscal Years 1999–2008: A Preliminary Update," Congressional Budget Office, July 15, 1998.

2. Scott Moody, ed., *Facts and Figures on Government Finance* (Washington, D.C.: Tax Foundation, 1998), p. 5.

to Medicare beneficiaries (hospitals, doctors, nurses, and so on).[3] In the total federal budget, approximately 47 percent of total spending consists of transfers of this sort.[4] So, to a large extent, decisions we make through governments about spending are not about the direct purchase of goods and services, but about the transfer of money from some taxpayers to others—who then, in turn, make their own decisions in the commercial market. But as a percent of total spending in the economy, government's share is quite significant.[5]

The simple arithmetic above, however, underestimates the importance of our decisions in the public sector because governments gain control over, or direct, resources in ways other than just spending. A specific instance is regulation. To see how this is so, think about the ways the federal government can acquire command over the resources it must have to operate. It can tax and then spend (the usual way). Or it can borrow and then spend. Or, simply print money and spend it on the resources it needs.[6] Fortunately, unlike some countries whose governments find themselves in distress, ours has not frequently resorted to the expedient of printing money. And, after decades of substantial

3. Unlike the Social Security program, the Medicare program is accompanied by significant government controls on health care providers.

4. *Budget of the United States Government, FY 1999* (Washington, D.C.: Government Printing Office, 1998), p. 341.

5. Another reason the proportion of GDP measure may overestimate the importance of collective decisions is that government is valued at input costs rather than at market prices, as in the private sector. To the extent government programs are more wasteful than those in the private sector, the measured GDP figures for government are inflated.

6. This works only because the federal government has a monopoly on the medium of exchange. Private money—once in widespread circulation throughout the nineteenth century and even for a short period during the Great Depression (for example, wooden nickels)—is unlawful.

deficit spending, it appears that, at least for a while, the federal government will have a balanced budget.[7]

But a fourth means of government's gaining command over resources is through the *conscription* of resources. There was a time in American history when governments required citizens to pay certain taxes "in kind," such as maintaining roads that ran by or through their property. Such direct forms of resource conscription are no longer used, save having to serve on a jury. Nevertheless, governments make widespread use of an indirect form of conscription known as *regulation.*

When government regulates the economy, it gains control over resources and directs them in ways they would not have been but for regulation. Reliable information on the overall cost of regulation is difficult to come by. Obviously, there are many problems of measurement. When the federal government forces a company to install "scrubbers" to reduce pollution emitted into the atmosphere, how much of this represents the extra cost of regulation versus costs the company would have incurred anyway, even without the federal control?

The direct *budgetary* costs associated with regulatory control are fairly easy to ascertain. According to a recent study by the Center for the Study of American Business at Washington University in Saint Louis, total federal outlays for U.S. regulatory agencies amounted to $18 billion in fiscal year 1998.[8] By contrast,

---

7. As conventionally measured by total receipts from all sources versus total outlays. This "cash budget" standard is misleading because it doesn't account for many changes in assets and, especially, liabilities. It is often said that if those in the private sector kept their books like those in the federal government, they'd end up in jail. (For more on such problems with the federal budget, see Miller, *Fix the U.S. Budget!: Urgings of an "Abominable No-Man"* [Stanford: Hoover Institution Press, 1994], chapter 10 and appendix.)

8. Melinda Warren and William Lauber, "Federal Regulatory Budgets and

measures of the *indirect* costs of regulation are considerably less precise. The estimates of the total regulatory burden prepared by Professor Thomas Hopkins of the University of Rochester suggest that the federal government's "conscription" of resources through regulation imposes costs on the economy upwards of $700 billion per year.[9] According to Richard Vedder, these estimates are low because they fail to take into account some of regulation's drag on productivity. He found that regulation lowers productivity growth more than 0.5 percent annually and that without two decades of regulatory drag (starting in 1963), total output of the economy would have been $1.3 trillion higher.[10] (See figure 1-1, which shows the total of federal, state, and local spending over the post–World War II years and, in addition, the costs of federal regulation in the latter years for which we have estimates.) As you can see, the total costs of government are significant and have generally risen over time. Currently, the total costs of government—actual outlays plus the costs imposed by regulation (including state and local)—amount to nearly half of total GDP.

Another way of visualizing the importance of our decisions in the public sector of the economy is by the following thought experiment: on average, what portion of the year do we work for the government, and what portion do we work for ourselves? As we all know, whether we like it or not, the government has first

---

Staffing, Fiscal Year 1999," Center for the Study of American Business, Washington University, August 1998.

9. Thomas D. Hopkins, "Regulatory Costs in Profile," Center for the Study of American Business, Washington University, August 1996. Similar results were found by John F. Morrall. (See U.S. Office of Management and Budget, *Report to Congress on the Costs and Benefits of Federal Regulation,* 1997.)

10. Richard K. Vedder, "Federal Regulation's Impact on the Productivity Slowdown: A Trillion-Dollar Drag," Center for the Study of American Business, Washington University, July 1996.

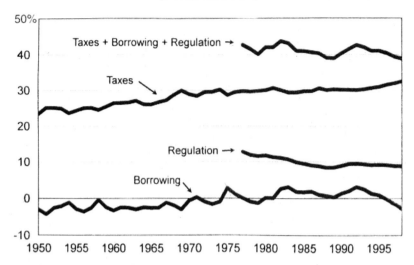

FIGURE 1-1. Total Cost of Government (as percent of GDP). (*Sources:* Tax Foundation and Thomas D. Hopkins, "Regulatory Costs in Profile," Center for the Study of American Business, Washington University, August 1996.)

claim on our income—that's what withholding is all about. So, assume that during the first part of the year we work for government, and after satisfying its demands we work for ourselves.

The Tax Foundation, a nonprofit, nonpartisan organization that has been in existence for more than fifty years, has compiled just such a statistic, called "Tax Freedom Day" (figure 1-2). As you can see, in 1998, on average, people in the United States worked until May 7 just to pay taxes.[11] Of this total, they worked until March 29 to pay federal taxes and another forty-one days (that is, through May 10) to pay state and local taxes. Alternatively, we might think of what portion of the *day* we work to pay taxes and what portion we work for ourselves. According to the Tax Foundation, in 1998 we worked two hours and fifty minutes

11. Patrick Fleenor, Scott Moody, and Stephen Shelby, "Tax Freedom Day 1998 is May 10," Tax Foundation, April 1998.

FIGURE 1-2. Tax Freedom Day. (*Source:* Tax Foundation.)

out of a typical eight-hour work day to pay federal, state, and local taxes, leaving five hours and ten minutes for ourselves.[12]

Of course, spending and regulation are not the only ways our decisions about government affect our material well-being. Those in that shrinking pool of people who lived through the Great Depression remember well the demands that government *do something* about unemployment, deflation, and other sources of misery. What they didn't know at the time—few people did—is that government itself contributed to the problems by inept management of the money supply and the imposition of many programs that, while well-intended, actually slowed the recovery. Over time economists have developed a more sophisticated un-

12. In keeping with the concept of cost described above—where the real cost of government is the sum of direct outlays and regulatory costs—Americans for Tax Reform has begun to compile a record of when, on average during the year, we leave off paying for government through taxes, borrowing (the two of which, of course, add up to spending) *and* regulation, and start realizing income for ourselves. They call this "Cost of Government Day." (See Americans for Tax Reform, "Cost of Government Day: June 25, 1998.")

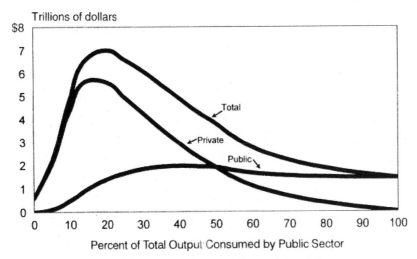

FIGURE I-3. Economic Output versus Relative Size of Government

derstanding of how the economy works, and public policy is much more likely to minimize downturns and to enable prosperity than in decades past.

Our decisions about government affect our well-being in less direct, but possibly more important, ways. Take our choice of the overall tax rate. Important work by a number of scholars suggests that tax rates pose a substantial (net) drag on the economy. The usual conclusion is that if the relative size of government were smaller, the economy would grow much faster, increasing the overall material well-being of society.

As the relative size of government (ratio of economic output commanded by government to total output, expressed as a percent) increases, total output at first rises and then falls (see figure 1-3). The reasons are straightforward: at a stage of anarchy, output is low, but as property rights are secured, as contracts are enforced, and as rights to persons are protected, economic output expands; however, as government (in both relative and absolute terms) grows further, it reduces total output through suffocating regulations, tax policies that blunt incentives, other confiscatory measures, and outright waste. Also, the relative size of government can't increase forever without so penalizing total output that the absolute size of government falls.

In keeping with the available evidence (more on that below), figure 1-3 implies that total output tends to peak when government commands approximately 20 percent of output. By definition (with government at this point a growing fraction of the total), output consumed by the private sector peaks at a lower level of government. And, in keeping with current theory and some limited evidence, resources devoted to government tends to peak at around 45–50 percent of output.

Using U.S. data for the period 1949 to 1989, Gerald Scully found that the "optimal" (that is, growth-maximizing) tax rate for the U.S. government would have been 22 percent instead of the observed 35 percent. If this tax rate had prevailed over the period, the rate of economic growth would have been 5.6 percent instead of 3.5 percent; total wealth created would have been $76.4 trillion instead of $29.9 trillion; and tax revenue would have been $17.5 trillion instead of $13.8 trillion.[13] Scully's conclusions are in accord with similar research based on U.S. data by Peter Grossman, Edgar Peden, and Richard Vedder and Lowell Gallaway.[14] Richard Rahn, Harrison Fox, and Lynn Fox ana-

13. Gerald W. Scully, "The 'Growth Tax' in the United States," *Public Choice*, 1995, pp. 71–80. He found similar results for New Zealand: "Taxation and Economic Growth in New Zealand," *Public Policy Review*, 1996, pp. 1–9.

14. Peter J. Grossman, "The Optimal Size of Government," *Public Choice*, 1987, pp. 193–200; Edgar A. Peden, "Productivity in the United States and Its Relationship to Government Activity: An Analysis of 57 Years, 1929–1986," *Public Choice*, pp. 153–73; Richard Vedder and Lowell Gallaway, "The Impact of the Welfare State on the American Economy," Joint Economic Committee of the U.S. Congress, December 1995; and Vedder and Gallaway, "Government Size and Economic Growth," Joint Economic Committee of the U.S. Congress, December 1998. See also James Gwartney, Robert Lawson, and Randall Hol-

lyzed a variety of developed countries and concluded from this international comparison that the growth-maximizing size of government is much lower—on the order of 10 percent.[15] A few other scholars found contrary results, concluding that the optimal size of government might well be larger.[16] Either way, there is strong evidence that the overall size of government and its command over resources affect the economy in a significant way.

The degree of freedom we choose for government to bestow on the private sector matters too. For example, in a study published by the Heritage Foundation and the *Wall Street Journal*, Bryan Johnson, Kim Holmes, and Melanie Kirkpatrick found a strong *positive* relationship between the degree of economic freedom in a country and that country's rate of economic growth. For example, they found that long-run average annual per capita economic growth was 2.88 percent for countries whose economies are "free," 0.97 percent for those whose economies are "mostly free," −0.32 percent for those whose economies are "mostly unfree," and −1.44 percent for those whose economies are "repressed."[17] They also found a positive relationship between the degree of economic freedom a country gives to its private sector and the wealth of its citizens (as shown in figure 1-4).[18] Similarly, Gerald Scully found that in societies with free and

combe, "The Size and Functions of Government and Economic Growth," Joint Economic Committee of the U.S. Congress, April 1998.

15. Richard W. Rahn, Harrison Fox, and Lynn H. Fox, "Economic Growth and the Optimal Size of Central Government," Rockville, Md., Citizens for Budget Reform, April 13, 1997.

16. See, for example, Rati Ram, "Government Size and Economic Growth: A New Framework and Some Evidence from Coss-Section and Time-Series Data," *American Economic Review*, March 1986, pp. 191–203.

17. Brian T. Johnson, Kim R. Holmes, and Melanie Kirkpatrick, *1999 Index of Economic Freedom* (Washington, D.C.: Heritage Foundation, 1999), p. 10.

18. Ibid., p. xxix.

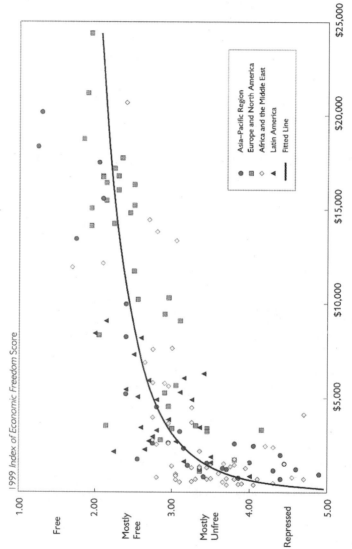

FIGURE 1-4. Economic Freedom versus Standard of Living. (*Source:* Brian T. Johnson, Kim R. Holmes, and Melanie Kirkpatrick, *1999 Index of Economic Freedom* [Washington, D.C.: Heritage Foundation, 1999], p. 10. Reprinted by permission.)

open political systems the standard of living (per capita income) rises (on average) 2.53 percent a year versus 1.41 percent for those that don't. In those societies that have a basic rule of law, the standard of living rises 2.75 percent a year versus 1.23 percent for those that don't. In societies that recognize property rights, the standard of living rises 2.76 percent per year versus 1.10 percent for those that don't. And, finally, in those societies that have all three attributes, the standard of living rises on average 2.73 percent versus 0.91 percent for those lacking those attributes.[19]

So whether we are talking about just the size of government or whether we broaden the discussion to include the major policies and institutions that government establishes and within which the economy operates, it is undeniable that the decisions we make about government have a significant influence on our standard of living. Just how we go about making those decisions is the subject of the rest of this book.

OUTLINE OF BOOK

This book is about political markets—how we select our representatives, how they interact with one another, how closely the outcomes of the political process conform to our preferences, and what reforms, if any, would seem warranted. In discussing the theme of this book with others, I've usually found it useful, and in some cases necessary, to contrast political markets with commercial markets. Because they are so ubiquitous, people relate easily to commercial markets. Moreover, they recognize the im-

19. Gerald W. Scully, "The Institutional Framework and Economic Development," *Journal of Political Economy*, 1988, pp. 653–62. See also Scully's *Constitutional Environments and Economic Growth* (Princeton: Princeton University Press, 1992) and Zane A. Spindles, "Liberty and Development: A Further Empirical Analysis," *Public Choice*, 1991, pp. 197–210.

portance of competition in these markets and would not stand for the kinds of anticompetitive behavior that is so often observed in political markets. Accordingly, in chapter 2, I set forth how commercial markets are organized, starting with the principle of consumer sovereignty and how we all "vote with our pocketbooks" to choose goods and services and how producers respond to these demands. We'll also get into the basic regulatory framework faced by industry, specifically the antitrust laws and other rules affecting the competitiveness of industry. As we shall see, the performance of commercial markets, while not perfect, is quite good.

Chapter 3 provides an introduction to political markets. Because of its importance, because of data availability, because of the abundance of research in the area, because most people are more familiar with this market, and because of its clear-cut anticompetitive features, the federal legislature is the subject of most of the examples and analysis. We as voters choose agents to represent us in political markets much as we choose firms to supply us with goods and services in commercial markets. Candidates compete for our votes, just as firms compete for our dollars. We voters get to choose a number of representatives (for example, senator, governor, and member of the local city council), just as we consumers get to choose different goods and services (for example, shoes, computers, and automobiles). Political markets operate within a regulatory framework analogous in some tenuous ways to the antitrust laws and other laws affecting competition. As we shall see, political markets are less competitively organized and tend to perform less well than commercial markets.

Political markets are characterized by certain basic differences with commercial markets that make it more difficult for them to be organized competitively and for them to perform as well as commercial markets. The more salient differences are addressed in chapter 4. First is the fact that the agent is chosen by majority or plurality vote and therefore (especially in the event your candidate loses) is not likely to reflect all of your preferences. Nor will the decisions made on your behalf necessarily be the ones you would have chosen. Second is the fact that representatives serve fixed terms—whereas in commercial markets you may switch to another provider instantly if you're not happy with the relationship. Related to this problem is the so-called principal-agent problem, which simply means that the interests of your representative may not always coincide with *your* interests and that the representative has a certain amount of discretion to follow her interests rather than yours. Finally addressed is whether political markets can be as efficient in meeting the demands of voters as commetcial markets are in responding to the needs of consumers—and what effect competition has on the efficiency of political markets.

Chapter 5 addresses *the* major institutional restraint on competition in political markets, which is the *contrived* advantage enjoyed by incumbents. Many have pointed out that incumbents have a significant advantage over challengers, but most of this literature has failed to distinguish between the *natural* advantages enjoyed by incumbents and those they themselves have erected to ward off challengers. Also, most of the work has been related to the question of "fairness" instead of the effects of incumbents' advantage on efficiency. Using the federal legislature as the major example, we get some notion of the advantage held by incumbents in terms of the assets of office, including their use of the franking privilege and the constituent services they provide, leading to more direct contact with voters and subsequent debts of gratitude purchased at taxpayer expense. Incumbents are also advantaged by having a federal election law that limits the effectiveness of challengers to compete and in dealing with regulators, specifically the Federal Election Commission. We shall see also that incumbents at the federal level often work with state and local officials to generate other impediments to challengers. As a consequence of these advantages—some natural and some contrived—it is accurate to apply the appellation *monopoly politics* to political markets in this country.

What do we do about the scourge of monopoly politics? Many reforms have been advanced, the first of which is the "throw the bums out" approach, whereby voters are encouraged to elect someone else if the incumbent doesn't perform well. I also explore a number of the institutional changes that have been proposed, including term limits. The revisions commanding the most public comment today, however, come under the rubric "campaign finance reform." Thus, in chapter 6 we examine some of the major proposals of this type that have been advanced either in Congress or in the press. Each is judged by the simple criterion of what effect would these changes have on the competitiveness of the political marketplace?

Conclusions and recommendations are contained in chapter 7. First, there is a summary of the work and a description of the lessons learned. On this basis, a set of recommendations is offered that would improve the competitiveness of political markets, as well as a specific plan of action.

The results of this work are contrary to the accepted wisdom that to "clean up politics" all we need do is to drive money out of the system. In fact, the amount of money in the system appears reasonable compared with advertising expenditures in the private sector. To the degree that the money in politics might be deemed excessive, it reflects the power of politicians to bestow favors on, or penalize, various groups of citizens. They have amassed this power by designing laws that grant them a major franchise to "do good" and get reelected at taxpayer expense and have protected this power by designing institutions to insulate themselves from challengers. Thus, the solution is not to drive money out of the system but to reform the political marketplace to make it more competitive and more responsive to the voters.

CHAPTER TWO

Competition in Commercial Markets

We make decisions in commercial markets by "voting with our pocketbooks." That is, we choose from a broad offering of goods and services, or we save for future consumption. The choice is ours.

CONSUMER SOVEREIGNTY

The organizing principle of commercial markets is that the consumer is king. The consumer is the boss. As the first modern economist, Adam Smith, noted around the time our country was founded:

> Consumption is the sole end and purpose of all production, and the interest of the producer ought to be attended to, only so far as it may be necessary for promoting that of the consumer.[1]

1. Adam Smith, *An Inquiry into the Nature and Causes of the Wealth of Nations* (New York: Modern Library, 1937), p. 625. The original was published in 1776.

This idea of the primacy of the consumer in commercial markets is sometimes referred to as "consumer sovereignty."[2]

Think of it this way: there's a vast array of resources in the economy available for producing goods and services. Just what gets produced, when, and who receives them are questions answered by consumers using their dollar "votes." If you decide to buy a computer rather than a TV set, you in essence notify the retailer, who notifies the wholesaler, who tells the producer there's an order for one more unit. The producer then "assembles" more resources to produce the computer you want (or replace the one you took from the shelf in the retailer's store). Simultaneously, by your decision to purchase a computer rather than a TV set, you are telling the retailer, the wholesaler, and the producer that one less TV is demanded. That producer, in turn, reduces its requirement for resources. So the consumer not only gets to choose among offerings, but actually determines *what* gets produced, *when*, and *who gets them*.

Commercial markets are sometimes more complicated than just described, but the key principle is that relevant decisions are driven by the choices of consumers. Sellers (producers, wholesalers, retailers) vie with one another to cut costs and lower prices as an inducement to consumers to choose them over their rivals. They advertise in an effort to inform and persuade us of the superiority of their products or the services they provide. Some also develop and market entirely *new* products or services to attract our attention.

Some examples illustrate. Sellers (again, producers, wholesalers, retailers) of routine, standardized products and services are likely to "compete" on the basis of price. Therefore, they will

2. See William H. Hutt, *Economists and the Public: A Study in Competition and Opinion* (London: Jonathan Cape, 1936); and George H. Hildebrand, "Consumer Sovereignty in Modern Times," *American Economic Review Papers and Proceedings*, 1951, pp. 19–33.

work especially hard to reduce costs. Farmers are a good example. Since wheat (by grade) is standard, an individual wheat farmer can make more money only by reducing costs—or, what amounts to the same thing, increasing yield. As a general proposition, the more wheat an acre, the lower the average cost of wheat produced. As other wheat producers engage in the same type of behavior, the result is lower prices to consumers.

Where products or services are capable of being differentiated in the consumer's eye, sellers will stress the advantages of their offerings. Sometimes their advertising messages contain factual information, other times it is basically "fluff," and frequently it is both. Take advertising for fast foods. Burger King came out with the "Big King" to combat McDonald's "Big Mac." By and large the campaign stressed the features of the new burger and how these compared with the features of McDonald's offering. At the other extreme are McDonald's ads featuring their trademarked character, Ronald McDonald: to the extent there is information in these ads, the character and the jingle convey the message that dining at McDonald's is *fun*. Other ads by the company contain a mix of information (we have burgers, fries, "McRibs," and many other good things to eat) and fluff (if you bring a friend, you'll have even more fun).

Of considerable interest to economists has been whether advertising by firms in an industry actually increases sales overall or just the *market shares* of the various firms. The answer depends on the industry. Some goods and services are highly discretionary, and in such cases advertising by individual firms can expand total sales of the industry. An example is travel. This leisure good is highly responsive to advertising, in terms both of the industry overall and of the market shares of firms in the industry. By contrast, industries that produce goods or services that consumers purchase routinely are not as susceptible to the influence of advertising. Although beer producers (distributors and retailers) spend a lot of money each year advertising their products, there is little evidence that the overall industry advertising bill affects the volume of beer drinking. Rather, spending by individual firms affect the market shares of the firms doing the advertising.[3]

The development and marketing of completely new products and services are important, and easily underestimated, activities that are a reflection of consumer sovereignty. Just how important these activities are can be seen in a brief retrospective about common goods and services. The schoolgirl starts out the day eating a Poptart heated in a microwave oven, rides to school in a minivan, uses a small calculator to do problems in math, gets on the World Wide Web to find out about Jefferson's Monticello for a paper in history class, picks WordPerfect off the Microsoft desktop to use in typing her paper, listens to her disk player while working out in gym class, asks her teacher to send Grandma a fax of her latest homework paper on which she received an A, cruises the mall on the way home using her ATM card for cash to make a few purchases, snacks on Pringles, uses Dad's cell phone to call Lucy for the latest gossip, and watches MTV on satellite TV before going to bed. This story is unexceptional. But each of these products *didn't exist* (or weren't in widespread use) in the previous generation. They were developed and brought to market by producers who hoped consumers would buy them.

Sellers do not do all of this just to be good citizens. Rather, they do it primarily for the money. As Adam Smith noted,

> It is not from the benevolence of the butcher, the brewer, or the baker, that we expect our dinner, but from their regard to their own interest.[4]

3. See, for example, John E. Calfee, *Fear of Persuasion: A New Perspective on Advertising and Regulation* (Washington, D.C.: American Enterprise Institute, 1997), chapter 5.

4. Adam Smith, ibid., p. 14.

That the organization of the selling side of the equation is driven by self-interest should not come as a surprise or be criticized anymore than the organization of the consumption side is similarly driven. That is, the reason a consumer chooses a computer rather than a TV is that he feels this choice will make him happier (the product will be "more useful," will "better satisfy needs," or whatever) than the alternative. The reason the seller promotes a line of TV sets is in hopes of making a buck. The exchange makes both parties better off. The seller would rather have the money than the TV set. The consumer would rather have the TV set than the money.

That's not to say that sellers and consumers are always happy campers. A seller may work hard, take significant risks, and it simply because consumers won't buy the product or service it offers. Even sellers who stay in business are constantly in danger of being muscled out of the way by sellers that better satisfy consumer wants, often by developing new products or new services that consumers prefer. This is the essence of competition: consumer choice constantly forces business to offer the best product or service at the lowest possible price. And it forces sellers to innovate to anticipate consumer demand.

Of course, consumers may want products or services that no one produces. Or what they want may be available but the price may be exorbitant. For example, I'd like a notebook computer that weighs no more than three pounds, is no more than one inch thick, runs at least 300 MHz, and has a full-size keyboard, an active matrix screen, a built-in floppy *and* CD-ROM, a five-GB hard drive, at least 96 MB of RAM, and a built-in battery that lasts at least five hours between charges—all for a price of $1,000. Any takers? Not now—no product on the market meets these specifications and certainly not at the price—but, with firms aggressively competing for consumers, in just a few years, who knows?

INCENTIVE TO MONOPOLIZE

The discussion thus far presumes that markets are organized *competitively*. If this isn't the case, the results are not the same. Although economists have a lot of technical definitions of monopoly,[5] the basic notion is that anyone or anything that comes between a willing consumer and a willing seller impairs the efficiency of the marketplace.

The traditional case is where a firm, or group of firms, acquires an ability to exclude other (actual or potential) sellers from the industry. In the extreme case, suppose that you are the only seller in the industry and rivals are excluded. Depending on how reliant consumers are on the product or service you sell, you may be able to raise prices far above those that would prevail in a competitive market. You may be able also to lower costs by reducing the quality of the product or service you offer and find that the reaction of consumers is "tolerable." By doing so, you may be able to earn a much higher return on your investment than if you were in a competitive industry.

Consumers have a similar incentive to crowd out "competitors" for the attention of sellers. They can organize and bargain as a unit, putting sellers "at their mercy." For a while, at least, such *monopsonists* (term economists use to describe monopoly power on the part of consumers) can force sellers in a competitive

---

5. Many such definitions are based on the *effects* of monopoly power: price exceeding marginal cost, existence of price discrimination, and so forth. It is important to note that "monopoly" is not synonymous with "bigness," though there is some confusion over this point generally. (For example, according to a *USA Today*/CNN/Gallup poll, 32 percent "completely agree" and 45 percent "mostly agree" with the statement "There is too much power concentrated in the hands of a few big companies." [*USA Today*, December 8, 1998, p. 2B].) A small industry may possess monopoly power, and a large industry may be vigorously competitive.

industry to charge lower than competitive prices or increase the quality of the product or service they sell or both. Since sellers will experience losses, they will exit the market unless some accommodations are made. That's one reason why monopsony has not been a burning issue and why most public concern is directed to monopoly power on the selling side.[6]

Impediments to competition on the selling side are not limited to the extreme case where, for whatever reason, there is just one seller and other potential sellers are excluded. Suppose there are three sellers, but no more are allowed. If these three are permitted to collude and can work out a plan among themselves and enforce it, the result will be as inefficient as in the case of a single seller who is able to exclude all potential competitors.

Left to their own devices, sellers will seek to form alliances, exclude rivals, and behave monopolistically. As Adam Smith observed long ago,

> People of the same trade seldom meet together, even for merriment and diversion, but the conversation ends in a conspiracy against the public, or in some contrivance to raise prices.[7]

Since sellers know that collusion seldom works for long and that in making such attempts they open themselves to criminal prosecution, they frequently turn to government for protection from competition, if not an outright grant of monopoly franchise.[8]

---

6. The major reason, of course, is that the costs of organizing hundreds, thousands, or even millions of consumers and having them "police" their behavior (that is, to keep some consumers from cheating on others by purchasing more than allowed) are very high.

7. Adam Smith, ibid., p. 128.

8. It is interesting that Adam Smith did not devote even more of his tract to efforts by industry to seek the state's aid in suppressing competition. After all, the genesis of his *Wealth of Nations* was to show that the mercantilist (protectionist) policies of the British government were based on a false premise,

ANTITRUST LAWS

A series of statutes called "antitrust laws" has evolved over the past century to limit monopoly power in American business. Firms and industry associations all work within this framework and are generally familiar with its prohibitions.[9] The rules are pretty much summed up in the mandate

> Thou shalt not collude with others to limit competition, nor shall thou engage in monopoly behavior such as price discrimination and tying arrangements, nor shall thou engage in unfair acts or practices such as defrauding or deceiving consumers.

Specifically, the Sherman Act of 1890 made unlawful all contracts, combinations, and conspiracies to restrain trade. It also made anyone who monopolized, or even attempted to monopolize (or otherwise combine or conspire to restrain competition), guilty of a felony. Although enforcement of the act was limited until the early part of this century, it laid down the gauntlet to those who would limit consumer choice by creating monopoly power. It was a *felony*, and those who engaged in such activity were *felons* and subject to criminal sanctions.

Two more major antitrust statutes were enacted in 1914, partly out of concern that the Sherman Act was not sufficient to deal with monopoly behavior. The Clayton Act prohibited price discrimination, a policy whereby monopoly firms could extract more *consumer surplus* from customers by charging different prices to different classes of customers, where such differences

---

namely, that a nation's wealth is enhanced by excluding imports and acquiring gold or silver.

9. For a concise summary of the statutes and their history, see John H. Shenefield and Irwin M. Stelzer, *The Antitrust Laws: A Primer* (Washington, D.C.: American Enterprise Institute, 1996).

are not based on differences in costs but on how much consumers in the different classes are willing to pay. A local mechanic, for example, might charge a person passing through town more for a car repair than he does a local resident because (in economists' terms), the out of towner's demand is "less elastic." Such a practice would be roundly condemned. But what if a medical doctor charges indigents less than the well-to-do? Both are unlawful under the spirit, if not the letter, of the Clayton Act.

Using the same logic, the Clayton Act also outlawed arrangements whereby a firm seeks to extract more from consumers by tying one product to another. One celebrated case involved IBM's punch cards. In the 1950s and early 1960s, IBM was the only major provider of computers, and the mechanism for entering data utilized cardboard stock about 3.75 inches by 7.25 inches in which holes were punched by a machine. IBM would sell (or lease) you a computer, but only if you agreed to purchase the card stock from them. By having a relatively high markup on the card stock, IBM was able to price discriminate by, in effect, charging a higher margin for computer use by those with less elastic demands.

The Clayton Act also made it possible for the federal government to block anticompetitive mergers *before* they took place. That tool was later amended by the Celler-Kefauver Act and the Hart-Scott-Rodino Act, the latter of which set up an elaborate timetable requiring merger partners to notify the federal government of their intentions well in advance and to submit significant information detailing the nature of their combination and its effects on competition. The rationale was that it is easier to prevent a merger that might ultimately prove anticompetitive than to "unscramble the eggs" after such a merger has been consummated.

The other antitrust statute enacted during 1914 was the Federal Trade Commission (FTC) Act which established an agency headed by five commissioners to research and comment on the overall competitiveness of industry and to act on its own to improve the vitality of competition in the economy. The commission was given a broad mandate to prohibit "unfair means of competition and unfair or deceptive acts or practices." Generally, the "unfair means of competition" language has been interpreted as giving the FTC the authority to enforce the other antitrust statutes, including the Sherman Act.[10] The commission uses the "unfair or deceptive acts or practices" language to prosecute firms that engage in "rip-offs" and other frauds (such as boiler room phone banking to bilk unsuspecting people out of their savings) and to hold firms accountable for the truthfulness of their advertising messages.

As a practical matter, the commission doesn't intervene when the advertising message is technically false so long as it is mere puffery ("Old Sour Hops beer is better than all the rest—and it'll put hair on your chest!"). Nor will the commission intervene when the product or service is relatively low in price, when consumers purchase it frequently, and when they can judge for themselves reasonably well the validity of the claims made by the seller. Examples include pencils, fast foods, wines, and shaving cream. But when the item is high in price, when it is purchased infrequently, and when consumers are unable to judge sellers' claims for themselves reasonably well, the commission may require advertisers to prove their claims are valid. Not only that, the commission may require that firms have "prior substantiation" of their claims—that is, have proof that their claims were true *before* they made them. Examples include automobiles, weight-loss programs, and medical devices.

---

10. Since the FTC can impose only civil, not criminal, penalties, it usually refers cases of price-fixing and other instances of collusion directly to the Antitrust Division of the Department of Justice for prosecution.

To many, the antitrust laws are the linchpin of capitalism. As former Justice Thurgood Marshall wrote in an opinion, "Antitrust laws in general, and the Sherman act in particular, are the Magna Carta of free enterprise."[11] No doubt the antitrust laws can serve a useful function; without them monopoly would be more widespread. But the enthusiasm of the antitrust advocates needs to be tempered by a realization that even without the antitrust laws competition would be the norm, not the exception.

Without government sanction, attempts to monopolize a market almost always fail. Collusion over pricing and market divisions falls apart because it is difficult for the firms to police each other and because firms have strong incentives to cheat. Firms will agree on a price and to limit sales, yet as soon as they get a chance, one or more of the conspirators will begin discounting or improving product or service quality to attract more customers. Even if collusion works for a while, new firms, attracted by high profits, are likely to enter and undercut the agreement. Because sellers are relatively small in number, tend to know their rivals, and can communicate with each other efficiently, monopolization by sellers is more likely to be successful than monopsony by consumers. But history has shown that sellers' efforts to restrain trade are seldom successful without help from the government.

The successful monopolies have been those where an industry has obtained a government franchise—and immunity from the antitrust laws. This is especially true of transportation. During the second half of the nineteenth century, the railroads expanded dramatically but were unable to realize monopoly power because each time they established minimum rates the cartel fell apart. In despair, they turned to the federal government, which obliged by establishing the Interstate Commerce Commission (ICC) in 1887.

---

11. *U.S. v. Topco Associates, Inc.*, 405 U.S. 596 (1972), para. 20.

Ostensibly set up to assure reasonable, nondiscriminatory rates and services, the Commission's real work was to enforce published rates and prevent "ruinous competition" among railroads. When the interstate trucking industry began to undercut the railroads' cartels in the early 1930s, rather than declare victory and close down the ICC, Congress brought truckers (and barge carriers) under the regulatory umbrella and had the agency enforce an even wider cartel. In the late 1930s, air carriers petitioned the federal government for protection against "unfair competition," and the result was the Civil Aeronautics Board (CAB), which managed and enforced a cartel among air carriers. In effect, over a 40-year period the government did what members of the transportation industry could not do—establish, maintain, and police a cartel.

Both the ICC and the CAB were disestablished by legislation enacted during the late 1970s and amended during the 1980s. As a result, the interstate transportation industry became remarkably more competitive, saving shippers and consumers literally billions of dollars per year. Yet monopoly power in transportation continues to exist, primarily in some (regulated) *intra*state service—for example, the franchised taxi operations of large cities.

Other franchised monopolies exist, of course, including the distribution of electric power. But even this monopoly is under attack and its franchise withering away because of federal and state reforms. In communications, the trend has been toward demonopolization for some time. The celebrated AT&T antitrust settlement of 1981 opened the long-distance telephone market to competition. In theory, at least, the Telecommunications Act of 1996 will open local telephone service to competition. Likewise, competition is coming to cable TV, not only from competing cable companies but from satellite TV. Although franchised monopolies still exist and are likely to remain for some time, especially at the local level, the argument for competition (as opposed to monopoly) has carried the day. Nevertheless, it is clear that government can create, nurture, and protect monopolists if it so chooses.

That industry will seek government protection from competition should not come as any surprise: it is both effective and insulates the participants from antitrust liability. But businesses seek protection not only of the sort described above (where government establishes and enforces an industry cartel). Economists use the term *rent-seeking* to describe the gamut of ways firms seek competitive advantage through government.[12] For example, domestic industries will seek tariffs or quotas on imported goods or services. Failing to get an advantage of this type, they may seek to have government establish stringent safety or other quality standards—much as the Japanese have discriminated against U.S.-produced automobiles by requiring difficult-to-meet standards and inspecting imported cars aggressively.[13] Similarly, at the behest of local meat producers, the European Common Market established safety standards that effectively disallowed U.S. beef imports.[14] Such *general* rent-seeking activities are immune from antitrust prosecution since the courts have held that such advocacy is protected by the First Amendment.

12. The concept was first explored by Gordon Tullock. See his "The Welfare Costs of Tariffs, Monopolies, and Theft," *Western Economic Journal*, June 1967, pp. 224–32.

13. Reforms were part of the 1995 U.S.-Japan Auto Agreement. See letter (and attachments) to U.S. trade representative Michael Kantor and U.S. secretary of commerce Ronald H. Brown from Japanese ambassador (to the U.S.) Takakazu Kuriyama dated August 23, 1995; available at http://www.ita.doc.gov/region/japan/usjfinal.html.

14. On August 19, 1997, a World Trade Organization (WTO) panel reported that the European Community's ban on meat from hormone-treated livestock was inconsistent with the WTO Agreement on the Application of Sanitary and Phytosanitary Measures. See WTO release of August 28, 1997, p. 2; available at http://www.wto.org/press/press75.htm.

Individual firms in an industry also have an incentive to obtain government help. Anything that lowers their costs, especially when their rivals don't get the same treatment, will increase their profits. A tax break not shared by others in the industry is a good example. The alternative of using government to raise rivals' costs can be equally effective.[15] If a firm can convince the government to require its rivals to meet more stringent safety requirements, issue warnings about its products, or subject them to lengthy investigations, the result can be a significant competitive advantage. For example, one of the oldest techniques on the books is for a firm to approach the FTC with confidential charges that a competitor is engaging in unlawful activity—in hopes the commission will at least investigate the charges and cause the target firm (or firms) to spend resources answering the inquiries. Better yet, the initiating firm hopes the Commission will find some violation and take issue with the company. Even if this only results in a "consent decree," the costs to the rival and the attendant bad publicity give the initiating firm a substantial competitive advantage.[16]

Thus, the antitrust laws are not perfect in protecting competition because they are capable of being used by businesses to limit competition. Even when there is no rent-seeking, the antitrust laws can be applied in ways that make competition less vigorous. For example, the general consensus among antitrust

15. There is an extensive literature on this subject, following the seminal work of Steven Salop and David Scheffman. See Steven C. Salop and David T. Scheffman, "Raising Rivals' Costs," *American Economic Review*, 1983, pp. 267–71.

16. A consent decree usually consists not of an admission of guilt by the investigated firm but of a promise by it not to engage in the challenged behavior in the future. Frequently, the agreement calls for the investigated firm to make annual reports to the FTC, just to prove it is not engaged in the challenged behavior—a recurring cost to the firm and a recurring advantage for the firm that initiated the complaint.

experts is that the Justice Department's case against IBM during the late 1970s was ill-founded, and many believe it lessened competition and slowed progress in the computer industry. Also, according to a Rasmussen survey, by more than two to one, people believe that the Justice Department constitutes a greater threat to competition in the computer software industry than Microsoft dominance.[17]

On occasion, the FTC has been even more aggressive and misguided. In the late 1970s, the FTC brought several cases contending that an industry dominated by several large firms (such as cereals) constituted a "shared monopoly" and should to be broken up. Furthermore, most antitrust scholars agree that FTC's record of enforcing the Robinson-Patman Act (the antidiscrimination act) has lessened competition and raised costs to consumers.

Thus, the regulatory framework within which competitors operate—the antitrust laws—is not perfect. It is capable of being abused by industries or firms seeking favors, and it is capable of being misapplied by federal enforcement officials. But the touchstone of the system is clear: competition is the law of the land; monopoly is clearly illegal. As we shall see, what's good for the goose (commercial markets) is not necessarily good for the gander (political markets).

17. Rasmussen Research release, "Has Bill Gates Done More for the Country Than Bill Clinton?" March 6, 1998. My own view of the matter is that there is enough evidence to warrant antitrust scrutiny of Microsoft's behavior. The relevant question, assuming liability, is whether the remedy fashioned by the courts would make this industry more competitive or less.

CHAPTER THREE

Competition in
Political Markets

In most political markets we choose people to *represent* us. They, in turn, choose the goods and services we get from the public sector (and, not incidentally, whether we go to war, what rules our commercial markets have to follow, and, within limits, the nature and enforcement of the rights and liberties guaranteed to us in the Constitution). At first blush, political markets (or "politics") seem very different from commercial markets (or "business"). Yet there are many similarities.[1] Those similarities are stressed in this chapter. The major differences are addressed in the next and subsequent chapters.

VOTER SOVEREIGNTY

In political markets we "consume with our votes," whereas in commercial markets we "vote with our pocketbooks." In political markets the voter is king, as with commercial markets the

---

1. For an early work commenting on the similarities (and some differences) between commercial markets and political markets, see Gary S. Becker, "Competition and Democracy," *Journal of Law and Economics*, October 1958, pp. 105–9.

consumer is king. Indeed, except for certain people in mental institutions and convicted felons, every citizen eighteen years or older has a right to vote.[2]

In theory, all votes are equal ("one man, one vote"), but that's not always the case. If you cast a ballot, your vote counts a binary one; if you don't vote, it counts zero. If you live in a congressional jurisdiction whose population (or, more specifically, voter turn-out) is less than average, your vote counts more than if you live in a jurisdiction with a population that's greater than average.[3] If you live in a state with a small population (for example, Vermont), your vote for U.S. senator ultimately counts more than if you live in a more populous state (for example, New York). If you vote in a "close" election, your vote is more likely to determine the outcome than if you vote in a one-sided contest. And if you are a "swing voter," not wedded to either party but voting the issues and the candidate, your vote is likely to count more than the vote of one who is.

Choosing a representative in a political market is very much like choosing a retailer in a commercial market.[4] The retailer is your "agent," supplying you with the goods or services you desire. When you go to Sears for a battery, you rely on Sears's good name and judgment to provide you with a reliable product at a good price. Sears is the agent for searching through the available product offerings and choosing a good line to carry. Likewise, when you go to the Winn-Dixie supermarket, you rely on the

2. See especially U.S. Constitution, Amendments XV, XIX, XXIV, and XXVI.

3. Each decade congressional districts are reapportioned. But because of indivisibilities (states with relatively small populations getting just a few members of congress) and because of uneven growth between reapportionments, districts often vary significantly in voting population.

4. To some extent the discussion in this section replicates points made in Donald Wittman, "Why Democracies Produce Efficient Results," *Journal of Political Economy*, 1989, pp. 1395–424.

chain to screen its products and offer you good value. An independent insurance agent whom you know and trust will choose among policy offerings the one that best suits you—or you may go to other "agents" such as Prudential or Travelers to provide you with the insurance services you need.

In political markets, you choose an agent to represent you in collective decision making. Old Charlie is a good fellow, makes sense, and will be effective; I'll vote for him. Old Charlie may hold views that are *close* to your own, but not exactly the same. But in commercial markets you have the same sort of problem. Going to Wal-Mart to buy an infant seat is a problem of choice. The store may have a good selection of colors, weight capacities, designs, and so forth. But the *exact* combination you prefer may not be available, so you have to choose among the best offered. Alternatively, you could shop at other stores or in the extreme make one yourself—just as you could offer yourself as a candidate if no Charlie, Louise, or Sam comes close to your views on the issues and is likely to be as effective as you think necessary.

In commercial markets we tend to gravitate toward enterprises that have earned our trust as agents. The local hardware store has gained our respect for having just the right gadget to fix a plumbing problem. We go there and rely on the clerk's advice with great comfort. We trust our doctors to prescribe the appropriate treatment. Even when we can judge reasonably accurately for ourselves the product or service as well as the price (perhaps armed with the latest issue of *Consumer Reports*, *Edmunds*, or *Stereo Review*), we tend to rely on a firm's reputation to deliver value. That's a major reason for franchises. You just *know* that the Dairy Queen five hundred miles from home will have hot eats and cool treats; that the Circuit City at Grandma's will have a nice Walkman; and that Allstate will have good car insurance when you relocate.

In political markets, the analogy to a commercial franchise is *a political party* and, to a lesser extent, an *interest group*. You may not know the views of the particular candidate, but the fact that he or she is a Democrat or Republican means something. It may mean even more if the candidate has secured the nomination of the party for the general election. Having limited time to research the candidates yourself, you are more than happy to rely on the label—Republican or Democrat—to guide you as you go into the voting booth. You also rely on the party to pressure the candidates to be true to their platforms once they are elected, just as you rely on Wendy's to take away the franchise of any of its restaurants that don't measure up.

You may also rely on endorsements or ratings by interest groups. If Americans for Democratic Action gives a candidate a high rating, that may be important to you. Or if the candidate is rated highly by the American Conservative Union, that may suggest this is a conservative you can trust. Other groups rate candidates on narrower issues. Where does the candidate stand on guns? Ask the National Rifle Association. Defense? Check ratings put together by *National Review* (which, by the way, is *not* an interest group). What about social issues? Try the Christian Coalition or the National Organization of Women. Consumerism? The Consumer Federation of America. Business? Call up the Chamber of Commerce of the United States or the National Federation of Independent Business. Organized labor? Look up the American Federation of State, County, and Municipal Employees. Trade or regulation? Ask Citizens for a Sound Economy Foundation.[5]

In both commercial and political markets those who would be

---

5. Tobias Ursprung found that the ratings of such groups have an ability to influence the outcomes of elections because voters remain rationally ignorant but do not want to vote "blind." See Tobias Ursprung, "The Use and Effect of Political Propaganda in Democracies," *Public Choice*, March 1994, pp. 259–82.

your agents solicit your support. In commercial markets it's called *advertising*. In political markets it's called *campaigning*. Just as firms seek your business by advertising their products, services, and prices, parties and candidates seek your favor by campaigning—telling you why you should choose them. Just as some advertising contains specific information—"The Macho Gym has the latest exercise machines and is staffed by qualified instructors"—some campaigning is highly specific—"I will vote *for* the new bridge; I will vote *against* the zoning requirement; and I will vote *for* two more schools." Just as some advertising is fluff— "Come to the Macho Gym and get in shape for the summer fun"—some campaigning is "fluff" as well; "I assure you, my fellow citizens, I believe in freedom and justice for all mankind."

Business firms devote considerable resources to product and service development. They may design a new product or service or simply make the basic one better. For example, Chrysler developed the minivan and improved it over the years by listening to consumer feedback on the basic design. In political markets, parties and candidates engage in a broad variety of efforts to make their offerings more appealing to voters. They may simply inform the public of the positions they take and combat misinformation generated by others, including opponents. Or they may engage a firm to do polling and interpret public opinion. Sometimes this leads parties and candidates to sharpen their messages (for example, which issues are more important and which are less, and how best to communicate the campaign's platform). At other times polling results lead parties and candidates to change their positions to better match the views of the electorate.

Political parties and candidates also develop new approaches to attract voters, commonly called "new ideas." The analogy with commercial markets is close. A firm may come up with a new, technological marvel, but that may not be enough. "Can we get it produced in volume?" "How do we market it?" and

"Will people buy it?" are among the questions that will be asked. In political markets a clearly superior idea such as eliminating price and entry controls in the transportation industry may be embraced only cautiously, if at all, because political agents find it difficult to "sell" the idea to the electorate. Especially vulnerable are good ideas that are capable of being demagoged by opponents, such as converting Social Security to a system of personal savings accounts ("My opponent wants to *destroy* the Social Security system and put old folks out in the street!"). This "new idea" enterprise ranges from the general to the specific: from the major (nonpartisan) think tanks, clustered mainly around Washington, D.C., to the various research efforts and retreats organized by the political parties, to the individual candidate's sitting down at the kitchen table, scratching her head, and musing, "Let's see, just what *would* be the best thing I could do for my constituents?"

Firms not only attempt to provide the "right" products and services currently available and develop new ones as well, but seek to provide them at the lowest cost. In political markets, parties and candidates not only take positions on issues to appeal to voters and develop new ideas, but try to deliver all this efficiently. Within practical limits (some dictated by "politics"), political agents promote the delivery of goods and services from the public sector at reasonable cost. Agents will rail against waste, fraud, and abuse. They will promise lower taxes or at least no tax increases. Or, if they acquiesce to higher taxes, they will justify their position by saying more revenue is needed to fund essential new programs. They will work to prioritize, cutting out less important programs (and thus lowering the overall cost of government) and focusing on those more urgent.

INCENTIVE TO MONOPOLIZE

These similarities between commercial markets and political markets are based in part on the existence of *competition* among agents. Firms compete for consumers' dollars; parties and candidates compete for citizens' votes. Consumers and voters are sensitive to what providers offer and will choose others if not satisfied. This *freedom to choose* is absolutely essential to making markets work effectively. Your right to go to K-Mart if Wal-Mart doesn't satisfy you keeps Wal-Mart on its toes. Your right to purchase a Ford rather than a Chevrolet helps keep General Motors focused on consumer preferences for automobiles. Your right to switch from Safeway to Giant Foods keeps Safeway working hard to earn your loyalty. In fact, the people most likely to change—those most sensitive to differences in the quality of service and price offerings of major vendors (sometimes called the "switchers") are the most important consumers in keeping markets competitive.

To no less extent, the freedom to choose among parties and candidates is essential to making them responsive to the electorate. Your right to switch allegiance from Carla Jones to Henry Smith is key to making Carla responsive to your preferences and making her effective in the delivery of public goods and services. Your right to abandon the Democrats for the Republicans keeps the Democrats attentive to the needs of voters (vice versa for Republicans). Your right simply to "opt out" and not vote at all keeps both parties on their toes. Just as in the case of commercial markets, where the switchers play a key role in assuring effective "representation," in political markets voters who are more "independent," who judge the issues and candidates for themselves, are more important than others in making the parties and candidates responsive to the electorate.

Just as in commercial markets, agents in political markets have an incentive to monopolize the marketplace. Business firms that exclude rivals can raise prices, diminish quality (and therefore reduce costs), make more profit, and in general live more comfortable lives, free from the hassles of having to "compete." Political parties and candidates who exclude rivals have much more power and influence, can more easily reject the interests of their constituents, have guaranteed tenure, and live easier lives. The goal is to exclude all rivals, from any source. Thus, parties want not only to persuade voters of the superiority of their stands on the issues and their candidates, but to limit the ability of rival parties to appeal to voters. Likewise, candidates not only want to gain the favor of voters, but want to limit the ability of any rival to command the attention of voters and gain their support.

To the extent that agents in either type of market achieve "dominance" by superior effort, there is no harm. It is said by some that Microsoft's dominance in the market for computer operating systems is due to its superior product and its marketing prowess. Ethyl's dominance in the market for octane boosters reflects its history of offering a product superior to those of its rivals. In political markets, to the extent that "one-party rule" is the product of superior issues, candidates, and campaigning, it is of no consequence. For example, to the extent the Democrats' dominance of Chicago politics reflects superior efforts to gain voter approval, the outcome should be of little concern. But to the degree it might be due to successful efforts to exclude rival parties and candidates, the voters of Chicago have been short-changed. Similarly for the Democrats' dominance of politics in most Southern states during the 1940s and 1950s, where winning the Democratic primary was tantamount to winning the general election, or to the Republicans' current dominance of politics in most mountain states.

The payoff to political parties and candidates from excluding rivals or colluding with them is not as easily seen or quantified as in the case of commercial firms, where the major part of the bottom line is higher profits. To the extent they can exclude rivals, political parties and candidates get their way on issues. The monopolizing party becomes more important and able to distribute more favors to its supporters than under a competitive system. Those who have the most to say about the positions on issues taken by the monopolizing party effectively have more control over the provision of public goods and services than the electorate in general. Candidates who can exclude rivals have an easier life. They don't have to work so hard. They can more often "vote their consciences," even when these positions conflict with those of their constituents. They don't have to worry so much about being displaced at election time by an insurgent challenger offering the electorate a superior choice. They are less likely to suffer the humiliation of being criticized by opponents.[6]

Absent an ability to exclude all rivals, political parties and candidates have an incentive to collude to suppress other potential parties and candidates. "Let's you and I fight it out; what we *don't* need is *another* party (or candidate) coming in." Thus, even by simple arithmetic, the odds of winning are better when there are two parties or candidates than if there were three or more. Even if the third (or fourth) party or candidate has little chance of prevailing, they can "upset the applecart," change established relationships between the two major parties or candidates, encourage the press and others to scrutinize their positions and performance more closely, and subject them to greater criticism.[7]

6. I am indebted to Eric O'Keefe, president of Americans for Limited Terms, on this point. O'Keefe argues that incumbents are prone not only to insulate themselves from competition but to snuff out criticism by opponents, even when such opponents have no chance of winning. (E-mail to me dated July 22, 1998, commenting on my working paper, "Incumbents' Advantage," mimeo, Citizens for a Sound Economy Foundation, December 17, 1997.)

7. The most important examples of recent times are Ross Perot's entry into

The voter is harmed if parties and candidates are successful in excluding all competitors or merely collude to share the spoils, just as the consumer is harmed by monopoly and collusion in commercial markets. The greater the exclusion of competitors, the greater the harm. Voters are likely to suffer greater harm when a political party or candidate is able to exclude all challengers than when they end up colluding with their major rivals, just as consumers are likely to be hurt more by being at the mercy of a monopoly seller than by having to deal with colluding rivals. The reason, of course, is that with rivals there is at least a choice and that collusion, even in political markets, tends to break down. Just as in commercial markets, political parties and candidates have an incentive to agree, but then to break the agreement. Only when such collusion is franchised and enforced by law is it as harmful to voters as when a single party or candidate is able to exclude all rivals.

ELECTION LAWS

As we saw in the previous chapter, competition in commercial markets has broad public support, and antitrust laws prevent monopoly. In political markets there is no direct analog to the antitrust laws, in part because most people haven't thought of the political process as constituting a market and because those who would make the laws preventing monopoly in political markets (that is, incumbents) have little incentive to do so. Nevertheless, some election laws do serve to preserve competition and prevent monopoly.

Of major importance are the constitutional guarantees and laws assuring voters the franchise. From locality to locality, from

---

the 1992 presidential race as an independent candidate and Jesse Ventura's election as governor of Minnesota as an independent candidate in 1998.

state to state, and across the nation, you can vote if you are part of the political jurisdiction. No party or candidate can interfere. (Of course, that's not to say there are no attempts to deny a person access to the ballot, or to deny voter discrimination along racial lines in the Old South, or the fact that for most of our nation's history women had no right to vote.) Just as one company can't hire goons to keep you from shopping at their rivals, parties and candidates can't limit your access to the ballot just because they suspect you'll vote for some other party or candidate.[8]

Federal law, for example, prohibits interference in elections for president, vice president, senator, and member of congress:

> Whoever intimidates, threatens, coerces, or attempts to intimidate, threaten, or coerce, any other person for the purpose of interfering with the right of such other person to vote or to vote as he may choose . . . shall be fined not more than $1,000 or imprisoned not more than one year, or both.[9]

Federal law also prohibits the buying of votes, the promising of employment opportunities in exchange for votes, and the use of other government largess (work relief, health benefits, contracts, et cetera) to influence voting in federal elections.[10]

Access to the ballot is another protection. As we will see in chapter 5, election laws tend to discriminate against challengers, but they assure that a determined challenger can put her candidacy before the voters. Most such laws simply provide that if the

---

8. Enforcement of the voter franchise and limits on intimidation are facilitated by the fact the ballot is *secret*. A interesting complication is Oregon's new provision for mail-in ballots, which are much more susceptible to influence. A similar problem obtains with absentee ballots: both can be "checked" by another party before submission.

9. U.S. Code, Title 18, Chapter 29, Sect. 594.

10. See U.S. Code, Title 18, Chapter 29, Sects. 595–607.

CHART 3-1. Market Analogies

Commercial Markets	Political Markets
Consumers	Voters
Franchises, trusted vendors	Political parties, interest groups
Advertising	Campaigning
Improving basic products and services	Better crafting and communication of basic message
Developing new products and services	Coming up with new approaches, new ideas
Attaining lowest cost	Fighting waste, fraud, and abuse
Achieving dominance through superior products and services	Achieving dominance through superior positions, candidates, effectiveness
Gaining dominance through efforts to exclude rival firms	Gaining dominance through efforts to exclude rival parties, candidates
Monopoly—harm to consumers	Monopoly—harm to voters
Antitrust laws to protect competition and constrain monopoly	No direct analogy, but voter franchise, ballot access and protections against voter fraud limit monopoly power

candidate meets certain qualifications, such as a threshold number of valid signatures of voters in the jurisdiction, she can get on the ballot, irrespective of party affiliation. In partisan races, a party can put a whole slate of candidates on the ballot by a similar procedure. The particulars differ from jurisdiction to jurisdiction, but the essential point is that a determined candidate or party wanting to participate in the market can do so. (Whether they can garner voter support is another matter.)

Laws against voter fraud and "stealing" elections also support competition and limit monopoly in political markets. Obviously, if an incumbent party or candidate had sole access to the ballots, the announced results might unduly favor the incumbent. Most jurisdictions have well-designed mechanisms to preserve the integrity of ballots and to assure an accurate count. This, of course, does not mean that voting fraud never occurs, but checks against voter fraud do limit this means of achieving monopoly power in political markets.[11]

There are many analogies between commercial markets and political markets (see chart 3-1). As will become increasingly clear, however, most political markets in the U.S. are analogous to industries in the commercial sector that operated as government-orchestrated cartels. For example, until the late 1970s the airline and trucking industries had to adhere to certain rules, but as long as they did they were immune from the antitrust laws. Although individual markets might have had more than one service provider, there was little real competition. And just as the deregulation of those industries saved consumers billions of dollars annually, reform of the political process would result in marked improvements in government performance.

---

11. Opportunities for voter fraud abound since in most jurisdictions a person doesn't have to present any identification in order to vote. This makes it easy for impostors to vote in the place of those who are deceased, who are convicted felons, or who have moved from the political jurisdiction. A variety of public-spirited organizations, such as the Voter Integrity Project, are involved in policing voter fraud.

CHAPTER FOUR

Unique Features of Political Markets

In the last chapter we explored how political markets are similar to commercial markets. But there are important differences. In this chapter we discuss several unique features of political markets and whether political markets can be as efficient in filling the needs of voters as commercial markets are in satisfying the needs of consumers.

INDIVIDUAL VERSUS COLLECTIVE DECISION MAKING

The principal difference between commercial markets and political markets is that in commercial markets decisions are made *individually* and in political markets decisions are made *collectively*. I purchase a Dodge Ram truck. You may prefer the more popular Ford F-150. Your neighbor may go for the "built-like-a-rock" Chevy. We all get to choose the truck that makes the most sense to us. Frankly, you care little what kind of truck someone else purchases. Even if they buy a Ford, there are many other Fords to go around. But if the three of us choose between two candidates for office and we three constitute the entire electorate, unless we're all in agreement one of us will be displeased with the outcome. In political markets you don't always get *your choice. This is the key difference between commercial markets and political markets.* In commercial markets, of all the choices available you get to choose the one that you prefer. In political markets, the choice you get may be the one you prefer, one that is "just OK," or even the one you *least* prefer.

The norm for modern democracies is to make choices by majority rule.[1] It need not be that way, and indeed we make many collective decisions with other rules. For example, in many states primaries and general elections require only a *plurality* (that is, getting more votes than anyone else) to win, not a majority of votes cast.[2] Also, Bill Clinton twice won the presidency with less than a majority of the votes cast (though with a majority of the votes of the Electoral College). The U.S. Constitution contains several provisions requiring *supermajorities* for actions to take place. For example, a presidential veto can be overridden but only by a two-thirds vote of *both* houses of Congress. Treaties require ratification by a two-thirds vote in the Senate. Ratification of constitutional amendments requires approval of three-quar-

---

1. Although rare, on occasion a popular election results in a tie, in which case other means may be utilized to resolve the outcome. See, for example, Rebecca Rowling, "Town Election Decided by Poker Hand," Associated Press, March 6, 1998.

2. In other cases, rules require runoffs between the top two vote getters in an election. Consider the case of Senator Paul Coverdell of Georgia. In 1992 he ran for the U.S. Senate. In the primary, he failed to get more than 50 percent of the vote and had to participate in a runoff, which he won. Then, in the general election, he failed to garner more than 50 percent of the vote against the incumbent, because the vote between the two was close and several minor-party candidates were on the ballot. Coverdell won that runoff too, having survived four "elections" in just a few months' time. (Coverdell won reelection to the Senate in 1998.)

Interestingly, following Coverdell's win in 1992, the Democrat-controlled legislature repealed the majority-vote requirement. In 1996, Democrat Max Cleland was elected U.S. senator with a narrow plurality. Had there been a runoff, he might well have lost since in runoffs the more conservative (usually GOP) candidate usually does better than in the general election.

ters of the state legislatures and so forth. In certain circumstances *unanimous* consent may be required for action in either house of Congress.

Candidates who hold views more or less in line with those of the greatest concentration of voters stand a better chance of winning, so "positioning" is a well-developed skill. An analogy with commercial markets illustrates. Enterprises have incentives to locate (in space or in quality dimensions, for example) close to potential customers. Imagine a beach where sunbathers are distributed evenly. Where will you set up your lemonade stand? Right in the middle of the beach! By doing so, you will place your stand where customer access is maximized. But if a competitor shows up, she will locate *in the same spot!* The reason is that if either of you move your location up or down the beach, the one who moves will lose customers to the one who stays put.

Harold Hotelling,[3] Anthony Downs,[4] Duncan Black,[5] and James Buchanan and Gordon Tullock[6] were among the first to apply the simple model of strategic location to politics (see figure 4-1). If the distribution of voter views across the spectrum, liberal to conservative, is even, then in a two-candidate race *both* candidates have an incentive to position themselves at midpoint X on the liberal-conservative spectrum—in order to maximize their chances of winning.[7] The reasoning is simple. If either candidate positions to the left or right of X and the other candidate stays

3. Harold Hotelling, "Stability in Competition," *Economic Journal*, 1929, pp. 41–57.

4. Anthony Downs, *An Economic Theory of Democracy* (New York: Harper and Row, 1957).

5. Duncan Black, *The Theory of Committees and Elections* (Cambridge: Cambridge University Press, 1958).

6. James M. Buchanan and Gordon Tullock, *The Calculus of Consent* (Ann Arbor: University of Michigan Press, 1962).

7. This assumes the candidates do not collude. If they do, then the model can yield different results.

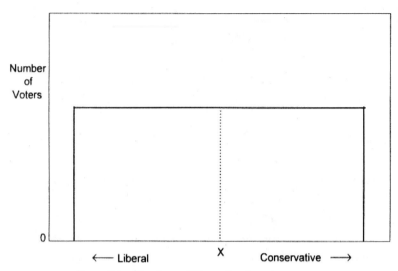

Number
of
Voters

0

←— Liberal   X   Conservative —→

FIGURE 4-1. Even Distribution of Voter Preferences

at X, the latter will clearly be the preferred choice of the majority of voters, coming closer to their positions.[8] Of course, this is a very simple construct. Voters may vary in the *intensity* of their views. If the "fringes" of the distribution are much more likely to vote—but only if the candidates come "close" to their views—whereas the voters in the "middle" are unlikely to vote at all, then candidates will maximize their chances of election by moving away from the center. By contrast, candidates may be able to "move" the electorate—through campaigning, for example. The candidate of a more liberal bent may be able to shift voters toward her view and win with a platform to the left of X. Or, for example,

8. I don't mean to imply that candidates slavishly tailor their views to those of the electorate. In fact, "integrity," combined with a realistic assessment of voter views, often discourages potential candidates from running for office. "I'm too conservative (liberal) to win in this district (state)" is a frequent refrain from would-be candidates. Whether we assume that candidates "position" themselves or that candidates emerge who hold the "right" views, the analysis is the same.

events (recession, threat of war, whatever) may shift the distribution of voter views to the right, and a conservative candidate may win with a platform to the right of X.

Moreover, voters are seldom one-dimensional in their attitudes. A common distinction is between "social" and "fiscal" issues. You might be a social liberal and a fiscal conservative or a social liberal and a fiscal liberal or a social conservative and a fiscal liberal or a social conservative and a fiscal conservative. Throw in more issues to consider such as spending more on defense versus spending less, being pro-gun versus pro–gun control, pro-life versus pro-choice, and pro-voucher versus pro–public school, and you can see how complicated and multidimensional the voting distribution can appear and how difficult it can be for candidates to position themselves so as to maximize their chances of winning—especially when their knowledge of the distribution is murky and the attitudes of voters keep changing.[9]

Distributions of voter attitudes are seldom as even or uniform as suggested by figure 4-1. Rather, they tend to look more like the normal, bell-shaped curve illustrated in figure 4-2. Rather than being uniformly distributed, there tends to be a "central tendency" of views. But as in the previous example, if there are two candidates both will locate at Y, the *median* of the distribution (also the *mean* in this example of a symmetrical distribution). If they position themselves either to the left or the right of the median voter's position, they will lose votes. This tendency of voting outcomes to reflect the position of the median voter is

9. In the case of multidimensional issue "spaces," in the simple competitive model in which a majority (rather than a plurality) is required to win, the outcome will reflect the views of the *mean* voter (in other words, the weighted-average voter) rather than that of the median voter (that is, the voter in the exact middle of the distribution). See Dennis C. Mueller, *Public Choice II* (New York: Cambridge University Press, 1989), p. 226. For our purposes here, the distinction is not important.

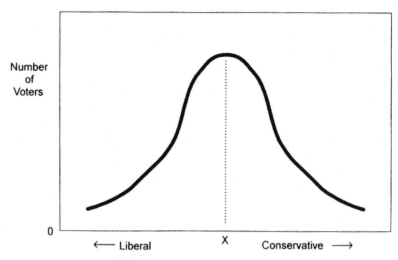

FIGURE 4-2. Normal Distribution of Voter Preferences

the major reason discussions of efficiency in collective decision making revolve around the likelihood that the median voter will best represent the views of the electorate—and why candidates work so hard to attract the support of the median voter.

Let's consider a few implications of this simple voting model, the most provocative of which is that as long as there are at least two candidates and majority rule you get the median-voter result. In the case of a single candidate, it really doesn't matter where he positions himself: he will win. Unlike the single vendor on the beach who earns more money by locating in the middle (maximizing his attractiveness to customers), the single candidate will win by default. With two candidates, each will adopt the position of the median voter. What about three or more? That's interesting. In the beach example, the emergence of a third vendor upsets the applecart but improves consumer welfare. At least as a starting point the customer-maximizing strategy for each of the three vendors is to locate in the middle of equal subsets of the distribution. One vendor will locate one-sixth of the way down the beach, another in the middle, and the third five-sixths the way down the beach. Although this solution is unstable (with vendors jockeying for position), having more than two vendors on the beach is of substantial benefit to consumers.

In this simple voting model candidates will position themselves in much the same way. If they are three in number, at least as a starting point they will divide the distribution into thirds and locate in the middle of their parts of the distribution.[10] Although the candidates may jockey for position, voters will have more choices, and the person for whom they vote is likely to be closer to their views than in the case of a single candidate or two candidates. But ultimately only one candidate can prevail. If there is a plurality rule, the result may or may not be the candidate holding the view closest to that of the median voter. But if there is a runoff *and* the candidates can reposition themselves, the result will be the view of the median voter.[11] Since candidates find it difficult to reposition themselves very far and remain credible with voters, in majority-rule situations there is a tendency for candidates to position themselves toward the views of the median voter in the initial round of balloting; while this strategy lessens their prospect of getting into the runoff, it increases their likelihood of winning if they do.

To sum up, in commercial markets consumers get their choice among the offerings, regardless of the preferences of other consumers in the market. Also, because the decisions of consumers are made individually (and their preferences are not all the same), new entrants can "win" in the marketplace by offering something

10. If there are *n* candidates, they will divide the distribution into *n* portions and position themselves in the middle of their respective portions.

11. By simple extension, you can see why candidates in primaries tend to hold the views of the median voters in their respective parties but also why, after winning the nomination, they tend to "move to the center." On this, see Mueller, ibid., p. 182.

different (or charging lower prices, for example). But in political markets, voters make decisions collectively, and the ultimate decision on a candidate (or the outcome of a referendum, for example) depends not only on the individual voter's preferences but on those of other voters. As long as there is choice among candidates and a simple majority is required to make the selection, the ultimate outcome is likely to reflect the views of the representative (or median) voter. As Dennis Mueller concludes,

> Competition for votes between candidates leads them "as if by an invisible hand" to platforms that maximize social welfare. The analogy between market competition and political competition does exist. Both result in Pareto-optimal allocations of resources.[12]

It would seem, then, that the collective decision-making feature of political markets does not derail the general observation that competition is efficiency enhancing—whether in commercial markets or political markets.[13]

FIXED TERMS AND
PRINCIPAL-AGENT PROBLEM

A second major difference between commercial markets and political markets is that in the commercial markets consumers may

---

12. See Mueller, ibid., p. 214. This construct, of course, presumes a reasonable *constitution* within which political competition takes place.

13. I have not discussed here the "intensity" problem—namely, that although a minority of voters might have a major stake on one side of an issue and the rest have only a nominal stake on the other side, the outcome of a majority vote (without trades) will be inefficient since the "cost" to the losers is much greater than the "gain" to the winners. Interestingly, voter turnout often solves this problem inasmuch as the minority in this example will have a keen incentive to vote, whereas the turnout of the majority will be low—the result being that the "minority" voters prevail at the ballot box.

switch between providers instantaneously, whereas in the political markets, once chosen, voters typically are "stuck" with a representative for a fixed term of office. As discussed in the previous chapter, the ability of consumers to switch between sellers keeps sellers on their toes. The right of consumers to change sellers instantaneously also facilitates the entry of new producers and new products and services. The producer of a new hybrid (gas and electric) automobile need not wait for a special "eligibility" date to offer it to consumers but may introduce it anytime.[14] Obviously, this is an advantage to consumers, as they get access to new products and services sooner rather than later. It is also an advantage to enterprising producers.

Elected officials are at all times free to deviate from their campaign platforms. To the extent they wish to seek reelection, they are likely to remain reasonably close to their previous positions— or at least take pains to explain to voters why their views have changed. The degree of discretion is fairly wide, however, because voters' "memory" is relatively short and unreliable. For example, John Mikesell found that state representatives tend to raise taxes early in their terms of office, relying on voter forgetfulness to save them come time for reelection.[15] Also, the freedom of agents to deviate from their platforms or the interests of their constituents is directly related to the length of their terms. Ryan Amacher and William Boyes found that as term length increases, legislators act more independently; they suggest that efforts to increase term length may be driven more by incumbents' interests in being free from their responsibilities to voters than by any desire to reduce election costs.[16]

---

14. Assuming it meets federal and state regulatory standards.

15. John L. Mikesell, "Election Periods and State Tax Policy Cycles," *Public Choice*, 1978, pp. 99–106.

16. See Ryan C. Amacher and William J. Boyes, "Cycles in Senatorial Voting

Of course, it is possible to replace a representative before the end of his term of office, but this is difficult. In some jurisdictions, the grounds for the recall of an official are limited. In most instances, the costs (usually a certain number of valid signatures on petitions) are prohibitive—and even then there is no assurance of success, as the offending representative may well win the recall vote. More often, replacement happens not from recall but from a resignation, usually as a result of scandal. Senator Bob Packwood was replaced by Senator Ron Wyden not as a result of a recall, but because Packwood's colleagues convinced him that resignation was better than suffering expulsion from the Senate. Speaker Jim Wright stepped down and left the House of Representatives because an ethics investigation was leading to censure and possible expulsion. Congressman Wilbur Mills gave up the chairmanship of the powerful Ways and Means Committee (and chose not to run again), not because he was recalled by his constituents, but because his relationship with the infamous Fanny Fox created enormous negative publicity and embarrassed his colleagues. Thus, while it is possible to secure the replacement of a representative during his term of office, such a procedure is costly and therefore rare.

Other mechanisms do exist for voters to "overrule" the decisions of their elected representatives, the most important being the option of placing issues directly on the ballot. Although there is no provision in the U.S. Constitution for a (national) referendum,[17] many states have such arrangements. In some instances, ballot measures can amend the state's constitution, in other cases they can have the force of state law, and in still other instances

---

Behavior: Implications for the Optimal Frequency of Elections," *Public Choice*, 1978, pp. 5–13.

17. The only way citizens can "overrule" the federal government is by having the states call a constitutional convention pursuant to Article V (which requires approval of two-thirds of the state legislatures).

the measures are advisory only. Such initiatives are properly viewed as ways citizens have around nonresponsive political agents—ways to circumvent or undercut monopoly politics.[18] Although there is increasing use of the device,[19] such mechanisms are cumbersome. Moreover, political agents—those in charge of establishing the rules to determine how many and what kind of measures get on the ballot—have an incentive to limit them or make them less substantive and thus less of a threat to their monopoly power.

Take, for example, Colorado's ballot rules.[20] To get a measure on the ballot, the initiator must get petitions signed by at least 5 percent of those voting in the most recent election for secretary of state. In 1994, however, the legislature passed (and the governor signed into law) *additional* requirements: (a) limiting the circulation period to six months, (b) requiring all circulators of petitions to meet age and residency requirements, sign affidavits, and wear identification badges, and (c) requiring strict reporting of all payments to circulators. The law was defended as necessary "to properly safeguard, protect, and preserve inviolate" the initiative process. The supposition might be that the measure was needed to put a stop to wasteful, trivial proposals that were being voted down by a disgruntled public. Yet in the period before passage of the reform the proportion of measures approved by the electorate was greater than the proportion approved after the

18. See, for example, Edward Felsenthal and Keith Perine," A Record Year for Ballot Initiatives," *Wall Street Journal*, November 5, 1998, p. B1; William Booth, "Initiatives Bypass Traditional Lawmaking," *Washington Post*, November 5, 1998, p. A33; and "Voters Reject Big Brotherism," *Washington Times*, November 5, 1998, p. A15.

19. See Felsenthal and Perine, ibid.

20. See, for example, decision of United States Court of Appeals for the Tenth Circuit in re *American Constitutional Law Foundation et al. v. Natalie Meyer et al.* (No. 94-1576) and *American Constitutional Law Foundation v. Natalie Meyer* et al. (No. 94-1581), 1997.

reform. Also, as one might predict, the average number of measures per year before the reform was larger than the number after enactment. In the five years before enactment of the reform, nine of the ballot measures called for limiting the powers of government or reducing taxes. After enactment, it took ten years—twice as long—to get that many such measures on the ballot.[21] Clearly, the effects of this "voter protection" measure were to strengthen the power of political agents and to limit voters' rights.[22]

This insulation from the electorate gives officials a great deal of latitude to follow their own interests rather than the constituent interests they were elected to represent. This is the classic principal-agent problem.

The previous chapter pointed out that in picking a seller in a commercial market a consumer is choosing an agent to represent them. That is, he or she is relying on that agent to secure the necessary resources and marshal them into the goods or services the consumer wants. The agent's discretion is highly limited, however. Knowing that the consumer has a right to change agents—instantaneously—the seller is unlikely to venture far from the interests of the principal (consumer) she represents.

---

21. See Colorado General Assembly, "Chronological Listing of the Number of Constitutional Amendments and Laws Voted Upon," available at www.state.co.us/gov_dir/leg_dir/lcsstaff/research/CONSTbL.htm.

22. In early 1999, the U.S. Supreme Court upheld the Tenth Circuit Court of Appeals' finding that provisions in the Colorado statute requiring that circulators be at least eighteen years of age, that they sign an affidavit (giving name and address), and that the circulation period be limited to six months were all constitutional but that provisions requiring petition circulators to be registered voters, that they wear name badges, and that the amounts they are paid be disclosed in periodic reports violates the First Amendment's guarantee of free political expression. Opined the court, "The restrictions in question significantly inhibit communication with voters about proposed political change, and are not warranted by the state interests (administrative efficiency, fraud detection, informing voters) alleged to justify those restrictions." See *Buckley v. American Constitutional Law*, 97-930, January 12, 1999.

Not so with the elected representative serving a fixed term.[23] The representative may safely ignore the interests of the median voter, at least to some extent, without fear of retribution. Often, a variance between the representative's action and the interests of his constituents is put down as "voting one's conscience." Such a rationale rings hollow, however, when such conscience is developed *after* the election. Moreover, elected officials often act in their own interests, whether to increase their compensation, champion their own pet causes, or, as we shall see in the next chapter, insulate themselves from competition.

POLITICAL SPEECH AND THE FIRST AMENDMENT

As discussed in chapter 2, there are certain restrictions on advertising in commercial markets. First, fraud and deception are unlawful under the antitrust laws (specifically, Section 5 of the Federal Trade Commission [FTC] Act). Moreover, the Lanham Act gives a seller a right to sue a rival who makes disparaging, *untrue* statements about his products or services. Accordingly, *comparative* ads in commercial markets are not prevalent.[24] A company doesn't wish to risk having the FTC challenge the veracity of its ads, knowing that rivals will be quick to complain to the authorities about any ads that hurt them. And they surely don't want to run the risk of having a rival sue for damages.

The situation is entirely different in political markets. There

---

23. In some representative democracies (for example, Canada and Great Britain) representatives may call "early elections"—before their fixed terms are up. This ameliorates, but does not eliminate, the principal-agent problem discussed here.

24. There are exceptions, of course. But the prevailing mode of advertising is to communicate information about the sponsor's product or service without (direct) reference to those of the sponsor's rivals.

are, and can be, *no* restraints on the content of campaign messages.[25] The reason is that the courts have held that political speech is protected by the First Amendment.[26] This gives rise to interesting differences in the behavior of competitors in the two markets. Deception seldom works in commercial markets because, if duped, a consumer can switch providers immediately.[27] But if an incumbent candidate is later caught lying or breaks promises, constituents have to wait until the next election, when the incumbent's insincerity may well have been forgotten. Thus, candidates have extraordinary discretion to deceive voters and to do so at will.[28]

Also, with insulation from legal liability, candidates have much greater discretion to engage in "negative campaigning." Richard Lau, for example, found that the electorate notices negative images more than positive images.[29] On the basis of a con-

---

25. As discussed in subsequent chapters, campaign finance laws have been held to impede the exercise of First Amendment rights. Roger Congleton argues that political advertising will tend to dissipate rents from holding political office and is thus wasteful to the extent such advertising fails to communicate relevant information about candidates or issues or both. See Congleton, "Rent-Seeking Aspects of Political Advertising," *Public Choice*, 1986, pp. 249–63.

26. On occasion interest groups do obtain preliminary restraints on the exercise of First Amendment rights. For example, in the final weeks of the 1989 and 1993 state elections, the Democratic Party of Virginia obtained lower court injunctions against the distribution of "voter guides" by conservative groups. Although these injunctions were later overturned on appeal, their purpose had been accomplished.

27. On the role of advertising in commercial markets, see John E. Calfee, *Fear of Persuasion: A New Perspective on Advertising and Regulation* (Washington, D.C.: American Enterprise Institute, 1987).

28. See Mikesell, "Election Periods"; Bruce T. Coram, "Why Political Parties Should Make Unbelievable Promises: A Theoretical Note," *Public Choice*, 1991, pp. 101–5; and Michael L. Davis and Michael Ferrantino, "Toward a Positive Theory of Political Rhetoric: Why Do Politicians Lie?" *Public Choice*, 1996, pp. 1–13.

29. See Richard R. Lau, "Two Explanations for Negativity Effects in Political Behavior," *American Journal of Political Science*, 1985, pp. 119–39.

trolled experiment on liberal arts majors, Gina Garramone found that if attack ads are conducted by independent groups they have a greater effect on the target and generate less of a backlash than do candidate-sponsored attack ads.[30] Using a similar technique, Brian Roddy and Gina Garramone found that viewers respond to *issue*-attack ads with a higher evaluation of the attacker (and a lesser likelihood of voting for the target) than do viewers of *image*-attack ads; they also found that the target's most effective response to an attack ad is a positive ad.[31]

Dan Johnson, founder of Illinois Citizens for Proportional Representation, summed it up this way:

> In winner-take-all elections, negative campaigning is very effective. Usually there are only two people running. Only one person can win. If I am a candidate in a winner-take-all race, if I can turn people off to my opponent and make them not want to vote for him, that is just as effective as getting them to vote for me. It is also a lot easier to try and attack my opponent to make her look bad than it is to convince voters to support me. It's easier just to run a commercial on television with frightening music in the background and distort my opponent's record than it is to talk about issues and policies.[32]

30. See Gina M. Garramone, "Effects of Negative Political Advertising: The Roles of Sponsor and Rebuttal," *Journal of Broadcast and Electronic Media*, 1985, pp. 147–59.

31. See Brian L. Roddy and Gina M. Garramone, "Appeals and Strategies of Negative Political Advertising," *Journal of Broadcast and Electronic Media*, 1988, pp. 415–27. Scott Thomas found that negative ads by challengers would increase the effectiveness of advertising by incumbents seeking to bring back their base. See Scott J. Thomas, "The Negative Advertising Theory of Campaign Expenditures," in W. Mark Crain and Robert D. Tollison, *Predicting Politics: Essays in Empirical Public Choice* (Ann Arbor: University of Michigan Press, 1990), pp. 245–56.

32. Dan Johnson, "PR, Winner-Take-All, and Negative Campaigning," April 8, 1997, available at www.prairienet.org/icpr.

Because negative advertising is so effective—especially when engaged in by challengers—it is little wonder that attempts have been made to outlaw the technique. But such efforts run smack into the First Amendment's protection of free speech. Nevertheless, every so often Congress or some state legislature will try. For example, recently the state of New Hampshire enacted a law against "push-polling"—a technique for telling voters bad things about your opponent, often without "leaving any fingerprints."[33] It works like this: the voter answers the phone, and the caller says they are with the XYZ (fictitious name) polling company, doing a survey of voter attitudes about the such-and-such race. After a few routine questions, the caller asks questions such as: "Would your attitude toward [Candidate A, the opponent] be different if you knew he had a record of child abuse? Was kicked out of college for stealing exams? Had a dishonorable discharge from the armed services? Was having an affair? Et cetera. No matter how despicable, such "messages" are protected by the free speech provision of the First Amendment.

This does not exhaust the differences between commercial markets and political markets.[34] But these are the main differ-

33. House Bill 443, approved April 1, 1998; text available at www.state.nh.us/gencourt/bills/oldbills/97hbills/hb443.

34. For example, in commenting on a draft of this work on August 18, 1998, Congressman Billy Tauzin of Louisiana offered the following observations/questions:

- Generally, people are not as happy with politicians as they are with products or services—because for each choice of representative there are usually only two to pick from, whereas with products and services, the range of choice is usually quite broad.
- People are likely to be able to articulate in much more detail *why* they like one product or service over another whereas they will have difficulty discriminating between candidates—whether they *like* them may be more important than the positions they hold.
- People shop at stores, in part because they like what the store stands for; in political markets, FEC reports serve the same function—giving the

ences for our purposes here. Of greater interest is whether with these differences political markets are capable of being efficient—and whether more competition would help or hurt.

IMPLICATIONS FOR EFFICIENCY
AND COMPETITION

With these unique features, are political markets capable of being efficient? And, specifically, does competition enhance efficiency or make it worse? The first question is whether, in the abstract, the *decision-making rule* in political markets—majority vote—leads to efficient outcomes.

In (competitive) commercial markets, the "right" goods and services get produced by the "right" providers, and they are purchased by the "right" consumers. Given the distribution of income, the competitive market accomplishes what economists call *Pareto optimality*—that is, there is no change in the pattern of production or consumption that would make one consumer better off without making another worse off—and therefore wealth and income are maximized.[35] But does majority rule in political

---

voter a notion of the people supporting the candidate.
- People don't really care how a firm is financed (capitalized), but they *do* care how a candidate is financed.
- In commercial markets, people often, and inescapably, make a "statement" with their purchases—the car they drive, the clothes they wear—whereas in political markets, people don't have to share for whom they vote.
- Why do politicians "run against the system?"; you don't often see titans of industry condemning capitalism.
- On negative advertising: if fast food restaurants emphasized how unsanitary and unhealthy their rivals' products are (in the same way politicians and parties constantly denounce each other), no one would buy hamburgers!

35. This is a simplified view, for it begs the question of income distribution and assumes no market imperfections, which could complicate the analysis.

markets lead to Pareto optimality—or anything near it? And what about competition? Would opening political markets to more competition increase income and wealth, or would it do the opposite?

Assessments of the efficiency of political markets are mixed. One strain, which we might call the "Chicago view," holds that despite the collective decision making of political markets and certain impediments to exchange, political markets are quite efficient. The other strain, which might be called the "public choice view," holds that problems in decision making, the lack of accountability, and the understandable propensity of political agents to respond to incentives cause political markets to be quite inefficient. As will become apparent, part of the difference in assessment stems from differences in assumptions about what political markets do and what might constitute the "ideal" (that is, efficient) political outcome.

The late George Stigler, a University of Chicago economist and Nobel laureate, was among the first to point out that political competition resembles economic competition. He argued that little significance should be attached to majority rule, inasmuch as those in the minority can bring their influence to bear in other ways.[36] Stigler implied that the concentration of candidates into two parties is no more an indication of monopoly power than is dominance of an industry by just two firms. Stigler focused on ways voters have to get around unresponsive governments. For

---

Also, the analysis does not address the fact that the *constitutional framework* within which markets operate is determinative of how they perform. (See, for example, James M. Buchanan, "Has Economics Lost Its Way?: Reflections on the Economists' Enterprise at Century's End," Institute for Humane Studies at George Mason University, 1997.) The general proposition—that competition leads to efficiency in commercial markets—still holds, however.

36. George Stigler, "Economic Competition and Political Competition," *Public Choice*, fall 1972, pp. 91–106. Also see Stigler, "Economists and Public Policy," *Regulation*, May/June 1982, pp. 13–17.

example, local governments, and even state governments, have to perform reasonably well, or constituents will simply "vote with their feet" and move to a jurisdiction where the government is more efficient. By analogy with commercial markets, these "switchers" in political markets limit the ability of local (and state) governments to perform poorly. Stigler also argued that even a party with monopoly power in a political market will choose a platform matching the view of the median voter, much as a monopolist will produce a product or service attractive to consumers, though at a higher price.[37]

Thus, the basic argument of the Chicago view is that voters on the losing side of an election are not losers after all; they are just disadvantaged and have to pay a higher price to get the policies they prefer. According to Stigler,

> A minority that feels intensely the need for a particular policy can pay a sufficient price to obtain it even with normal, legal democratic procedures. The method of payment is primarily vote-trading: the minority may vote for programs it is less opposed to than the one it seeks, and if the minority becomes larger, the number of subcoalitions of the "majority" it must persuade to join it on the desired issue diminishes, and the cost of getting their support becomes less.[38]

For those who doubt the effectiveness of minority groups in extracting policies they prefer, Stigler pointed to the success of special interests in obtaining protections that benefit them (for example, cartel regulation, import relief, and occupational licensure) but harm others in the economy more. Thus, according to

---

37. Michael McKee found support for Stigler's hypothesis, inasmuch as in Ontario the level of per pupil spending is responsive to the power of Catholic voters. See Michael McKee, "Political Competition and the Roman Catholic Schools: Ontario Canada," *Public Choice*, 1988, pp. 57–67.

38. Stigler, "Economic Competition," p. 99.

this view, majority rule doesn't mean that one side "wins" and the other side "loses." Rather, all participate in the political market and have an effect on the outcomes. Elections are analogous to periodic changes in the distribution of incomes among voters. Your vote matters more or less, depending on whether you are part of the winning majority. But your vote still counts.

Another University of Chicago economist and Nobel laureate, Gary Becker, also argues that political markets are efficient—in his view because of competition among special interest groups for influence over government policy.[39] Becker argues that, contrary to the general proposition that policies promoted by interest groups slow the economy (a thesis most recently associated with the late Mancur Olson[40]), interest group politics actually preserves public policies that expand output. *However,* Becker's argument is based on interest groups' having no more effective access to the political process than ordinary citizens.[41]

The strongest proponent of the Chicago view is Donald Wittman, a professor of economics at the University of California at Santa Cruz.[42] Wittman argues that political markets work *as well as* economic (that is, commercial) markets. It is his view that

> democratic political markets are organized to promote wealth-maximizing outcomes, that these markets are highly competi-

---

39. See Gary S. Becker, "Public Policies, Pressure Groups, and Dead Weight Costs," *Journal of Public Economics*, 1985, pp. 329–47; also see his "Competition and Democracy," *Journal of Law and Economics*, October 1958, pp. 105–9.

40. Mancur Olson Jr., *The Rise and Decline of Nations* (New Haven: Yale University Press, 1982).

41. Becker, "Public Policies," pp. 344–5. Also see Timothy Besley and Stephen Coate, "An Economic Model of Representative Democracy," *Quarterly Journal of Economics*, February 1997, p. 102.

42. See Donald Wittman, "Why Democracies Produce Efficient Results," *Journal of Political Economy*, 1989, pp. 1395–424, and his book *The Myth of Democratic Failure: Why Political Institutions Are Efficient* (Chicago: University of Chicago Press, 1995).

tive, and that political entrepreneurs are rewarded for efficient behavior.[43]

Wittman argues that the principal-agent problem discussed above is no more an impediment to efficiency in political markets than in commercial markets. Candidates develop reputations they do not wish to squander; parties police wayward politicians; and incumbents fear losing the next election—all of which limit divergences between the agent's behavior and the preferences of her constituents.

Wittman also argues that voters have much more information about their agents and what they do than is commonly believed and that the deleterious effects of biased information have been overstated. Moreover, to the extent that the political process is used to redistribute wealth, such transfers are efficient.[44] Nor does Wittman believe that much inefficiency results because of divergences between what might be called the "efficient solution" in a choice among policy alternatives (where the sum of voter marginal evaluations equals the sum of their marginal tax rates) and the view of the median voter. As long as voter distributions are reasonably symmetric and tax rates are fairly uniform, the actual outcome of the political process is likely to be close to the efficient solution. Moreover, in contrast to commercial markets, Wittman argues that problems of regulation in the public sphere are likely

43. Wittman, "Why Democracies Produce Efficient Results," pp. 1395–96.

44. University of Chicago economist Sam Peltzman credits increased demand for wealth transfers—and government's efficiency in orchestrating such transfers—as the major reason governments have grown so rapidly in the past few decades. See Sam Peltzman, "The Growth of Government," *Journal of Law and Economics*, 1980, pp. 209–88. Peltzman also found that voters are highly rational in rewarding representatives for income growth and penalizing them for inflation. See Sam Peltzman, "How Efficient Is the Voting Market?" *Journal of Law and Economics*, 1990, pp. 27–63.

to be no more severe than problems associated with making and enforcing contracts in the private sphere.

Both sides in the controversy readily admit that *perfect* efficiency is not a reasonable goal—in either type of market. Just as no commercial market has been characterized by *perfect competition* (including perfect information), it is not reasonable to assume that any political market will be characterized by *perfect competition* either. Moreover, many commercial markets can be described as having "market imperfections"—impediments to a truly efficient allocation of resources owing to external costs, economies of scale, systematically biased information, and pockets of monopoly power. The relevant policy question, however, is whether governmental intervention could actually improve matters or would end up being counterproductive. By analogy, all recognize that it is inevitable that political markets will be characterized by similar flaws. The question is whether the political markets we observe approximate that standard of *feasible* efficiency or whether they fall short of that goal.[45]

The public choice view of the efficiency of political markets holds that, without a requirement for *unanimity* among members of the electorate, it is impossible to say with certainty that any outcome is Pareto optimal—that is, no other outcome would make any member of the electorate better off without making another worse off. While majority rule may yield results approximating the efficient outcome, there is no assurance of efficiency, and the degree to which the outcome does comport with the

---

45. For example, in a separate paper Besley and Coate describe irreducible sources of inefficiency in political markets. See Timothy Besley and Stephen Coate, "Sources of Inefficiency in a Representative Democracy: A Dynamic Analysis," *American Economic Review*, 1998, pp. 139–56. Also, it is worth noting that in his early contribution Becker opined: "I am inclined to believe that monopoly and other imperfections are at least as important, and perhaps substantially more so, in the political sector as in the marketplace." (See Becker, "Public Policies," p. 109.)

efficient outcome depends mightily on the "constitution" within which the voting takes place.

Moreover, as a practical matter government officials are allowed such discretion and are so responsive to perverse incentives that by any reasonable criterion political markets cannot be said to be efficient. Given the current institutional arrangements that characterize political markets, some even question whether more competition would have a positive or negative impact on overall performance.

The public choice assessment is not based on the common (and overdone) observation that bureaucracies are inefficient and the private sector does it better (though there is truth to the allegation).[46] Rather, it is that political agents are relatively unaccountable—they have great discretion and they use that discretion to further their own interests and so make political markets relatively inefficient in meshing the desires of voters with the resources available. For the most part the problem stems from the design of current institutions—problems that, for the most part, can be remedied—not a basic flaw in the notion of democratic majority rule.

The basic principle can be illustrated with the common observation that politicians are interested in "pork." The analytics are simple. If a member of Congress can persuade her colleagues to appropriate some item benefiting her constituents *and have taxpayers in general pay for it,* this is great deal. Even if the item in question (new highway interchange, federal building, welfare "demonstration program," or whatever) is of only marginal value to her constituents, it may still be a bargain. Roughly speaking, if the value of the item is worth only 1/435th of its cost, it

46. The simple logic is that measuring performance in the public sector is difficult and therefore accountability suffers, whereas in the private sector failure to achieve a reasonable degree of efficiency results in failure of the enterprise.

will be worth supporting. This logic holds whether the representative's motivation is just being a good agent for her constituents or whether her goal is to increase the likelihood of her reelection. Obviously, this logic plays out on a much grander scale, not just limited to pork. Moreover, representatives have incentives to get favors for interest groups that may support their reelection efforts, especially when they can couch their efforts in public-spirited terms such as strengthening national defense or assuring everyone a decent wage.

I know from personal experience that the phenomenon just described is true and pervasive. In 1985, when I made my rounds of Senate offices prior to my confirmation as President Reagan's budget director (1985–1988), I was often taken into a senator's private quarters and told about the importance of such-and-such a program to him or to his constituents. Sometimes it was alleged that the administration had previously assured him of support on his special interest and that he expected the same from me. Often, after confirmation, I would testify before some congressional committee and be berated for not being sufficiently tough on overall spending or some specific aspect (such as defense); on returning to my office I would find a call waiting for me from the offending member wanting to remind me that while she was a budget hawk, the programs in her district or state had clear and convincing priority.[47]

Obviously, if each representative behaves this way the result will be gross inefficiency, as appropriations are made whose value overall is considerably less than the costs. The problem, of course, is that the true costs are not borne by those making the decisions. And it is axiomatic that an artificially low price will lead to excess demand. That's why public choice theorists suggest that specific

47. For another insider's perspective on "pork," see David A. Stockman, "The Social Pork Barrel," *Public Interest*, 1979, pp. 3–30.

government programs be "priced" to users to the extent feasible.[48]

By and large, voters are not faced with the true costs of government. Surveys show that voters tend to underestimate the taxes they pay, in part because so many taxes are hidden.[49] For typical wage earners, these include the employer's part of Social Security and Medicare. For consumers generally, these include the plethora of excise and other taxes that are seldom noted. Voters are also relatively unaware of the costs they bear from other means of financing government: debt and regulation. At present the federal government is technically running a surplus, but by generally accepted accounting rules that apply to the private sector—rules that would require reserves for liabilities—the federal government is still running a substantial deficit. Because voters don't fully capitalize their obligations to pay off the debt when it comes due, they underestimate the cost of government and demand more of it than is efficient. A similar logic holds with the costs of regulation: To the extent these costs are hidden, voters will demand too much government.

The problems just described—and empirical research[50]—suggest that political markets are substantially less efficient than commercial markets. In a particular twist of logic, some public choice scholars, including Nobel laureate James Buchanan of George Mason University, have even gone so far as to conclude that, *given the present institutional arrangements,* competition in political markets actually harms efficiency.[51] In their view, the

48. See, for example, James M. Buchanan, *Fiscal Theory and Political Economy* (Chapel Hill: University of North Carolina Press, 1960).

49. See Stephen Gold, "Taxes, Taxes, Taxes All Around," *Washington Times,* April 14, 1997, p. A17, citing surveys by the Bureau of Labor Statistics.

50. See, for example, the brief discussion in chapter 1 concerning the relationship between the relative size of government on the one hand and the rate of economic growth (or per capita income or wealth) on the other.

51. See James M. Buchanan, "A Defense of Organized Crime?," in Simon

existence of monopoly power, while leading to "excess profits" to parties and candidates in the form of some waste and lack of accountability, reduces the overall demand for government. In their judgment, the waste due to monopoly rents is less than the waste due to excessive government that would ensue with a more competitive political market.

These are provocative results. One line of assessment argues that political markets are indeed very efficient, contrary to the generally accepted notion (among economists, at least) that efficiency in the public sector pales in significance to efficiency in the private sector. The other line of assessment agues that political markets are significantly less efficient than commercial markets— and that, contrary to common sense, more competition in political markets would reduce efficiency, not increase it.

What is one to make of this? The Chicago view's rosy assessment is predicated in part on the existence of viable competition in political markets. Take away the competition, and those holding that view would lower their assessment of the efficiency of those markets. The public choice view's critical assessment is predicated on a number of institutional arrangements that lead to waste. Reform those features, and those holding that view would raise their assessment. Moreover, even without such changes it is not clear to me that increasing the competitiveness of political markets would have an adverse effect on efficiency. Political markets today resemble less pure monopoly than they do the regulated cartels in transportation before deregulation. There, limits on entry, on pricing, and on services resulted in substantial waste. The limited "competition" that did prevail in

Rottenberg, ed., *The Economics of Crime and Punishment* (Washington: American Enterprise Institute, 1973), pp. 119–32; and Geoffrey Brennan and James M. Buchanan, *The Power to Tax: Analytical Foundations of a Fiscal Constitution* (Cambridge: Cambridge University Press, 1980).

these markets furthered waste in some sense, but with the advent of price, entry, and service deregulation the transportation markets become much more efficient. Similarly, with institutional reforms, as well as more competition, political markets can become much more efficient.

CHAPTER FIVE

Incumbents' Advantage

For competition in political markets to be vigorous and have its intended, positive effects on efficiency, there must be a reasonably level playing field. Specifically, challengers must have an opportunity to compete. This is not to suggest that competitors be artificially limited. Indeed, you want the *natural* advantages of the candidates to shine through, whether these be a more popular platform, superior organizational abilities, outstanding good looks, first-rate communications skills, or even the name recognition that goes with having won previous races or being a celebrity. What you want to avoid—and what restrains the efficiency of the political marketplace—are *contrived* advantages for certain competitors. You want everyone to have an equal *opportunity* to offer themselves as a candidate, while preserving the natural advantages for candidates, whether they be incumbents or challengers.

Unfortunately, in most political markets incumbents have enormous contrived advantages over challengers, making the market considerably less competitive than ideal. This is especially true of contests for representation in the U.S. Congress.[1]

ASSETS OF OFFICE

Just how do members of Congress insulate themselves from competition? In a variety of ways. First are the contrived advantages that stem from their holding office. Members of Congress provide themselves with privileges such as free mail, telephone, Internet access, and web pages.[2] They pass ambiguous laws and promote complicated regulations in part to increase the demand for constituent service—which only they can provide, usually through taxpayer-funded caseworkers at various home offices in the district or state. They hold "town meetings" in their districts or states and generate other events to command press coverage. For the cost of franked mail, both in total and the average for members of Congress, see table 5-1, which also shows the number of House and Senate staff and the proportion in district or state offices. (Both the base and the proportion are rising, indicating that the typical member has a growing presence in the district or state.) For the growing complexity of laws and regulations with which people have to cope and with which members of Congress offer to be of assistance, see table 5-2.

Empirical evidence suggests that these assets of office, espe-

1. Incumbency is not an advantage in every respect. For example, an incumbent has a record to defend whereas a challenger may not be so encumbered. Just as it is easier to write a book review than it is to write a book, it is easier for a challenger to attack an incumbent's record than for an incumbent to defend her record. Also, if the mood of the country is "negative," owing, say, to economic recession (Bush) or to a failure of foreign policy (Carter), the electorate may turn out the incumbent "on principle."

2. When governments join the "digital revolution," elected officials typically commandeer for themselves the initial expenditures (web pages, e-mail, et cetera). See Cindy Crandall and Jeff Eisenach, *The Digital State, 1998* (Washington: Progress & Freedom Foundation, 1998).

TABLE 5-1. Selected Data for Congress

Fiscal Year	House Staff in District	(In Percent)	Senate Staff in State	(In Percent)	Cost of Franked Mail (in thousands of dollars)	Cost per Member (in thousands of dollars)
1980	2,534	(34)	953	(25)	$50,707	$95
1981	2,702	(36)	937	(26)	52,033	97
1982	2,694	(36)	1,053	(26)	75,095	140
1983	2,785	(37)	1,132	(28)	93,161	174
1984	2,872	(39)	1,140	(29)	117,277	219
1985	2,871	(38)	1,180	(29)	85,797	160
1986	2,940	(44)	1,249	(33)	95,700	179
1987	2,503	(33)	1,152	(28)	91,423	171
1988	2,954	(40)	1,217	(31)	82,163	154
1989	2,916	(39)	1,200	(31)	85,262	159
1990	3,027	(40)	1,293	(31)	87,945	164
1991	3,022	(42)	1,316	(31)	43,088	81
1992	3,128	(41)	1,368	(32)	62,762	117
1993	3,130	(42)	1,335	(32)	26,201	49
1994	3,335	(45)	1,345	(32)	53,109	99
1995	3,459	(48)	1,278	(30)	28,054	52
1996	3,144	(43)	1,290	(31)	34,023	64
1997	3,209	(44)	1,366	(31)	24,415	46

SOURCES: Norman S. Ornstein, Thomas E. Mann, and Michael J. Malbin, *Vital Statistics on Congress, 1997–1998* (Washington, D.C.: Congressional Quarterly, 1998); and U.S. Postal Service.

cially the provision of casework, confer a substantial advantage on incumbents. For example, of the top twenty in the House of Representatives, eleven spent more on franked mail than their challengers spent on their entire campaigns.[3] Morris Fiorina also found that the franking privilege benefits incumbents and in addition found that incumbents respond to narrow elections by

3. Data sources: National Taxpayers Union and Federal Election Commission. The point about the incumbent's spending on franked mail versus the challenger's spending on his entire campaign was noted in Steve Symms, "Campaign Finance Reform Gainers," *Washington Times*, August 13, 1997, p. A14.

TABLE 5-2. Federal Laws and Regulations (number of pages)

Year	Congress	Enacted Statutes	Federal Register	Code of Federal Regulations
1981			63,554	107,109
	97th	4,343		
1982			58,493	104,938
1983			57,703	105,654
	98th	4,893		
1984			50,997	111,830
1985			53,479	105,935
	99th	7,198		
1986			47,418	109,509
1987			49,654	114,337
	100th	4,839		
1988			53,376	117,440
1989			53,821	122,090
	101st	5,767		
1990			53,618	126,893
1991			67,715	125,331
	102d	7,544		
1992			62,919	128,344
1993			69,684	132,228
	103d	7,542		
1994			68,107	134,196
1995			68,108	138,186
	104th	6,369		
1996			69,368	132,121

SOURCE: Norman S. Ornstein, Thomas E. Mann, and Michael J. Malbin, *Vital Statistics on Congress, 1997–1998* (Washington, D.C.: Congressional Quarterly, 1998).

increasing their allocations to casework.[4] Albert Cover and Bruce Brumberg found that members of a control group receiving franked mail had a higher opinion of the incumbent than those who didn't.[5] Diana Evans Yiannakis found that constituent ser-

4. Morris P. Fiorina, "Some Problems in Studying the Effects of Resource Allocation on Congressional Elections," *American Journal of Political Science*, 1981, pp. 543–67.

5. See Albert D. Cover and Bruce S. Brumberg, "Baby Books and Ballots: The Impact of Congressional Mail on Constituent Opinion," *American Political Science Review*, 1982, pp. 347–59.

vice is especially effective in attracting supporters of the incumbent's challenger.[6] George Serra and Albert Cover found that constituent service creates a positive evaluation of the incumbent and has the most impact on constituents where only a small portion of them identify with the incumbent's party.[7] And, finally, George Serra and David Moon found that voters respond to constituent service and provocatively implied that, to some extent, constituent service can offset policy differences between the incumbent and his constituents.[8]

Members of Congress intimidate[9] major contributors to support them, not their opponents, and use Federal Election Commission (FEC) financial reports to police their behavior. (By reviewing the reports an incumbent will *know* just who is supporting her challenger.[10]) For example, in response to a letter requesting a contribution to a candidate challenging an incumbent, I received from a major trade association (which shall go nameless) the following reply (in part): "Our by-laws preclude us from providing support in primaries to non-incumbents." From personal experience in trying to raise money, I know that incumbents often remind major contributors that even if they

6. See Diana Evans Yiannakis, "The Grateful Electorate: Casework and Congressional Elections," *American Journal of Political Science*, 1981, pp. 568–80.

7. See George Serra and Albert D. Cover, "The Electoral Consequences of Perquisite Use: The Casework Case," *Legislative Studies Quarterly*, 1992, pp. 233–46.

8. See George Serra and David Moon, "Casework, Issue Position, and Voting in Congressional Elections: A District Analysis," *Journal of Politics*, 1994, pp. 200–13.

9. I use this term in the milder form of pressure and implied threat, not outright violation of criminal law.

10. Recently the process of policing contributors was made easier by the FEC's putting candidate financial reports on-line (available at http://herndon1.sdrdc.com/fecing/index.html). As further evidence on this point, note the large number of contributions challengers receive for $199 or $200, as candidates must report the names and addresses of all who contribute more than $200 in a calendar year.

lose, they will be around long enough to help them or hurt them.[11] Moreover, because of single-member districts (except in rare instances where redistricting reduces the number of representatives in a state), incumbents never compete with one another. On this, Randall Holcombe concluded:

> Thus, political markets are divided in the same way that cartels would divide markets in order to make each member a monopolist in his own territory to help enforce the cartel agreement.[12]

Incumbents also sneak district- or state-specific projects (that is, "pork") into appropriations measures and claim credit with constituents. For example, Robert Stein and Kenneth Bickers found that while most incumbents do not actively pursue pork, those who are most vulnerable to challengers do so aggressively.[13] Stein and Bickers also found that the success of incumbents in securing agency grants for their constituents influences potential challengers' deciding whether or not to enter the race.[14] Gerald Scully noted that since a congressman's ability to secure pork for his district is a function of tenure, constituents—especially in poor districts (for whom pork is more important)—have an additional incentive to return their incumbent to office.[15] Although the amount of pork is relatively small (less than 1 percent of total

11. This is one reason Political Action Committees (PACs) often give generously to incumbents who hold views antithetical to their interests while withholding support from like-minded challengers.

12. See Randall Holcombe, "A Note on Seniority and Political Competition," *Public Choice*, 1989, p. 287.

13. Robert M. Stein and Kenneth N. Bickers, "Congressional Elections and the Pork Barrel," *Journal of Politics*, 1994, pp. 377–99.

14. Kenneth N. Bickers and Robert M. Stein, "The Electoral Dynamics of the Federal Pork Barrel," *American Journal of Political Science*, 1996, pp. 1300–26.

15. Gerald W. Scully, "Congressional Tenure: Myth and Reality," *Public Policy*, 1995, pp. 203–19.

TABLE 5-3. Federal Pork Spending

Year	Amount *(in billions of dollars)*
1993	$6.6
1994	7.8
1995	10.0
1996	12.5
1997	14.5
1998	13.2

NOTE: A project is "pork" if it meets at least one of the following criteria:
- Requested by only one chamber of Congress
- Not specifically authorized
- Not competitively awarded
- Not requested by the president
- Greatly exceeds the president's budget request from the previous year
- Not the subject of congressional hearings
- Serves only a local or special interest

SOURCE: Citizens Against Government Waste.

federal spending), it is highly visible to constituents and is a growing phenomenon (see table 5-3).[16]

Incumbents distribute other "goodies" through a seniority system and through a system of committees, where the incumbent always has a leg up on any challenger. For example, Randall Holcombe found that senior legislators gain additional power by acting as brokers. He also found that the incumbency advantage is so valued that even members of the minority tend to preserve the status quo rather than trying for a majority.[17] Randall Bennett

16. Some pork is not "free." Alison DelRossi and Robert Inman found that members of Congress request fewer projects as the required amount of local funding increases. (See Alison F. DelRossi and Robert P. Inman, "Changing the Price of Pork: The Impact of Local Cost Sharing on Legislators' Demands for Distributive Public Goods," working paper 6440, National Bureau of Economic Research, 1998.) Also, on occasion, pork "backfires": Steve Stockman beat long-term incumbent Jack Brooks in 1994 in part because Brooks had been particularly greedy in getting pork for his district—so much so the behavior embarrassed his constituents.

17. Holcombe, "A Note on Seniority," pp. 285–88.

and Christine Loucks found that getting appointed to the House Banking Committee increases contributions from finance political action committees (PACs).[18] Christine Loucks found the same is true of getting appointed to the Senate Banking Committee.[19] Randall Kroszner and Thomas Stratmann found that committee members get more money from PACs with an interest in their jurisdictions and that the contributions increase with seniority.[20] Theodore Anagnoson found that during election years federal agencies speed up their approval of grants to the constituents of representatives who are on committees with authority over them.[21] Members have an incentive to preserve the "integrity" of the committee system because, with it, they wield more influence and raise more money. James Larue and Lawrence Rothenberg described a particular instance where Senate members voted against a measure simply because the proponent did an "end-run" around the relevant committee.[22] Mark Crain and John Sullivan found that for members of the majority party, incumbents assigned to committees having significant control over industries under their jurisdiction significantly increased their vote margins between the 1988 and 1990 elections.[23] Brian Roberts

18. Randall W. Bennett and Christine Loucks, "Savings and Loan and Finance Industry PAC Contributions to Incumbent Members of the House Banking Committee," *Public Choice*, 1994, pp. 83–104.

19. Christine Loucks, "Finance Industry PAC Contributions to U.S. Senators, 1983–88," *Public Choice*, 1996, pp. 219–29.

20. Randall S. Kroszner and Thomas Stratmann, "Interest Group Competition and the Organization of Congress: Theory and Evidence from Financial Services Political Action Committees," *American Economic Review*, 1998, pp. 1163–87.

21. See Theodore Anagnoson, "Federal Grant Agencies and Congressional Election Campaigns," *American Journal of Political Science*, 1982, pp. 547–61.

22. James Larue and Lawrence Rothenberg, "Institutional Features of Congressional Decisions: The Fight to Prohibit Smoking on Airlines," *Public Choice*, 1992, pp. 301–18.

23. See Mark W. Crain and John T. Sullivan, "Committee Characteristics

noted that the death of Senator Scoop Jackson (then chairman of the Senate Armed Services Committee) depressed the prices of stocks of companies in his state (Washington) and raised the prices of stocks of companies in the state of Georgia, home of Jackson's successor, Senator Sam Nunn.[24] Finally, Randall Kroszner and Thomas Stratmann found that one rationale for the committee system is precisely to increase contributions to incumbents from interest groups.[25]

In years when they have no effective opposition, potentially vulnerable incumbents amass "war chests" from vested interests and stand ready to spend same in order to intimidate would-be challengers. For example, David Magleby and Candice Nelson reported that "about 40 percent of the expenditures of the average major-party House candidate occur before the general election period . . . an advantage enjoyed by incumbents far more than by challengers."[26] Janet Box-Steffensmeier found war chests particularly effective in deterring high-quality challengers.[27] Even incumbents who aren't particularly vulnerable accumulate and hold onto campaign funds. At the end of the 1996 election cycle,

and Re-election Margins: An Empirical Investigation of the U.S. House," *Public Choice*, 1997, pp. 271–85.

24. See Brian E. Roberts, "A Dead Senator Tells No Lies: Seniority and the Distribution of Federal Benefits," *American Journal of Political Science*, 1990, pp. 31–58.

25. See Kroszner and Stratmann, "Interest-Group Competition and the Organization of Congress."

26. See David B. Magleby and Candice J. Nelson, *The Money Chase* (Washington, D.C.: Brookings Institution, 1990), p. 66. Significant expenditures "early" in the campaign for reelection reflect federal election rules that limit contributions to $1,000 *per cycle*—that is, once for the primary and then again for the general election. Incumbents facing no real opposition in the general election will frequently "campaign" on the primary cycle, then bank the general election funds.

27. See Janet M. Box-Steffensmeier, "A Dynamic Analysis of the Role of War Chests in Campaign Strategy," *American Journal of Political Science*, 1996, pp. 352–71.

for example, on average House challengers reported $4,792 cash on hand. For incumbents, average cash on hand was $175,872, and for incumbents who won with more than 60 percent of the vote, average cash on hand was $230,377. Some 156 incumbents had war chests exceeding $100,000; 97 incumbents had over $200,000; and 30 incumbents had war chests of $500,000 or more.[28]

Members of the same party collude by agreeing not to support any challenger in a primary, and members who do not have hotly contested races work for other incumbents—raising money for them and making personal appearances—expecting the same help in return if ever needed for reelection or for higher office. They also make sure a full menu of pork is available to incumbents who are in tight races.[29]

Incumbents work with their state legislatures and governors to redistrict in such a way as to protect, and possibly improve, their voting populations. David Gopoian and Darrell West found that incumbents were more likely to gain, rather than lose, from redistricting because legislatures tended to give incumbents of both parties a greater proportion of their party's voters.[30] To the extent there is a party bias in the redistricting process, it tends to

28. From calculations prepared by Parker Normann, based on data available from the Federal Election Commission.

29. Many of these efforts are orchestrated through and enforced by the respective parties' congressional and senatorial campaign committees. However, Mark Crain and Robert Tollison found that political parties are reluctant to make pork available to highly vulnerable colleagues because the flow of benefits from the public expenditure may accrue to a representative from the other party. See Mark Crain and Robert D. Tollison, "Pork Barrel Paradox," in W. Mark Crain and Robert D. Tollison, *Predicting Politics: Essays in Empirical Public Choice* (Ann Arbor: University of Michigan Press, 1990), pp. 59–78.

30. See David J. Gopoian and Darrell M. West, "Trading Security for Seats: Strategic Considerations in the Redistricting Process," *Journal of Politics*, 1984, pp. 1080–96.

favor the state's dominant party.[31] However, the partisan effects of redistricting tend to diminish over just a few election cycles.[32]

Incumbents also work to limit ballot access to third-party candidates. For example, Theodore Lowi concluded that state bans on "fusion tickets" (the nomination of the same candidate by more than one political party), sponsored by the major parties, have a simple objective: to eliminate competition.[33] James Hamilton and Helen Ladd found that ballot structure affects turnout (particularly for lesser-known candidates), party-line voting, and election results in heavily partisan districts.[34] For an idea of just how significant are the impediments to ballot access, see table 5-4.[35]

31. See Gary King, "Representation through Legislative Redistricting: A Stochastic Model," *American Journal of Political Science*, 1989, pp. 787–824; Janet Campagna and Bernard Grofman, "Party Control and Partisan Bias in the 1980s Congressional Redistricting," *Journal of Politics*, 1990, pp. 1242–57; and Bruce E. Cain, "Assessing the Partisan Effects of Redistricting," *American Political Science Review*, 1985, pp. 320–33.

32. See King, "Representation through Legislative Redistricting"; Peverill Squire, "Results of Partisan Redistricting in Seven U.S. States during the 1970s," *Legislative Science Quarterly*, 1985, pp. 259–68; and Richard Born, "Partisan Intentions and Election Day Realities in the Congressional Redistricting Process," *American Political Science Review*, 1985, pp. 305–19.

33. See Theodore J. Lowi, "A Ticket to Democracy," *New York Times*, December 28, 1996, p. A27.

34. See James T. Hamilton and Helen F. Ladd, "Biased Ballots?: The Impact of Ballot Structure on North Carolina Elections in 1992," *Public Choice*, 1996, pp. 259–80.

35. Also see Edward Felsenthal, "Minor Parties Are Campaigning against Curbs They Claim Condemn Them to Third-Class Status," *Wall Street Journal*, December 27, 1996, p. A8; and Richard P. Roberts, "Ballot Access for Third Party and Independent Candidates after *Anderson v. Celebrezze*," *Journal of Law and Politics*, 1987–88, pp. 127–81.

Even when reasonable, ballot rules can keep candidates from running. For example, Scott West, who polled 46 percent against Congressman David Obey in 1994 and had planned to take him on again in 1998, forgot to file his declaration of candidacy. (See *Roll Call Politics*, July 16, 1998, p.16.) A similar fate befell Ann Devore, who was the favorite to beat David McIntosh in the 1994 Republican primary. (McIntosh won the primary and the general elec-

TABLE 5-4. Congress: Getting on the Ballot, by State (S = Senate; H = House)

State	Filing Fee	Primary Access	Indigent Law?	Independent Candidate	Write-in?
Alabama	2% salary of office	File	Yes	1% voters	Yes
Alaska	$100	File	Yes	1% voters	Yes
Arizona	NA	0.5% party voters	—	3% voters	Yes
Arkansas	Yes	File	—	3% voters	Yes
California	2% salary (S); 1% salary (H)	65 voters (S); 40 voters (H)	—	3% voters	Yes
Colorado	2% salary (H)	NA	—	1,000 voters (S); 500 voters (H)	Yes
Connecticut	NA	Convention	—	1% voters	Yes
Delaware	Yes	File	Yes	5% reg. voters	Yes
District of Columbia	NA	2,000 party voters	—	3,000 or 1.5% reg. voters	Yes
Florida	7.5% salary	File	—	3% reg. voters	Yes
Georgia	3% salary	File	—	5% reg. voters	Yes
Hawaii	$75	$25	—	25 voters	No
Idaho	$250 (S); $150 (H)	1,000 (S); 500 (H)	No	1,000 voters (S); 500 (H)	Yes
Illinois	NA	5,000 (S); 0.5% last primary (H)	—	25,000 voters (S); 5% (H)	Yes
Indiana	NA	5,000 (S)	—	2% voters	Yes
Iowa	NA	1% party (S); 2% party (H)	—	0.5% party voters (S)	Yes
Kansas	Yes	NA	—	5,000 voters (S); 4% (H)	Yes
Kentucky	NA	2 party voters	—	5,000 voters (S); 400 (H)	Yes
Louisiana	$600	File	—	5,000 voters (S); 1,000 (H)	No
Maine	No	2,000 (S); 1,000 (H)	—	4,000 voters (S); 2,000 (H)	Yes
Maryland	$290 (S); $100 (H)	File	Yes	3% voters	Yes
Massachusetts	NA	10,000 (S); 2,000 (H)	—	10,000 voters (S); 2,000 (H)	Yes
Michigan	NA	1% vote for Sec. of State	—	1% voters (S); 2% (H)	Yes
Minnesota	$400 (S); $300 (H)	File	—	1% voters (S); 5% (H)	Yes
Mississippi	$300 (S); $200 (H)	File	No	1,000 (S); 200 (H)	No

State					
Missouri	$200 (S); $100 (H)	NA	—	10,000 voters (S); 2% (H)	Yes
Montana	1% salary	File	—	5% voters	Yes
Nebraska	1% salary	File	Yes	2,000 voters	Yes
Nevada	$500 (S); $300 (H)	File	—	1% voters	No
New Hampshire	$100 (S); $50 (H)	File	—	3,000 voters (S); 1,500 (H)	Yes
New Jersey	No	1,000 party (S); 200 party (H)	—	800 voters (S); 100 (H)	Yes
New Mexico	No	230 party (S); 77 party (H)	—	3% voters	Yes
New York	No	15,000 voters (S); 1,250 voters (H)	—	15,000 voters (S); 5% (H)	Yes
North Carolina	1% salary	File	—	2% voters (S); 4% (H)	Yes
North Dakota	No	3% voters or 300 voters	—	2% voters (S); 4% (H)	Yes
Ohio	$100 (S); $50 (H)	1,000 party (S); 50 party (H)	No	2% voters (S); 4% (H)	Yes
Oklahoma	$1,000 (S); $750 (H)	File	—	2% voters (S); 4% (H)	No
Oregon	$150 (S); $100 (H)	File	—	NA	Yes
Pennsylvania	$200 (S); $150 (H)	2,000 (S); 1,000 (H)	No	2% voters	Yes
Rhode Island	No	1,000 (S); 500 (H)	—	1,000 voters (S); 500 (H)	Yes
South Carolina	1% salary	File	No	5% reg. voters	Yes
South Dakota	No	1% party vote for governor	—	5% reg. voters	No
Tennessee	No	25 voters	—	5% reg. voters	Yes
Texas	$4,000 (S); $2,500 (H)	File	—	5% reg. voters	Yes
Utah	0.125% of total term salary	File	—	5% reg. voters	Yes
Vermont	No	500 party voters	—	5% reg. voters	Yes
Virginia	2% salary	0.5% reg. voters	—	5% reg. voters	Yes
Washington	1% salary	File	—	5% reg. voters	Yes
West Virginia	1% salary	File	—	5% reg. voters	Yes
Wisconsin	No	2,000 (S); 1,000 (H)	—	5% reg. voters	Yes
Wyoming	$200	File	No	5% reg. voters	Yes

NA = Information not available or unknown.

NOTE: Unless indicated otherwise, variable requirements (such as 0.5% of registered voters to gain ballot access in Virginia) refer to the state or district for Senate and House, respectively.

SOURCE: Karen M. Markin, Ballot Access 2 (Washington, D.C.: Federal Election Commission, 1995).

These state laws restrict competition from third parties and so protect both parties and candidates from competition. In some cases state laws are more direct in protecting incumbent candidates. For example, in Virginia incumbents have preferential power over the method of nomination: Incumbents who were nominated by means of a primary in the previous election may demand a primary (as opposed to a convention) in the current cycle. Louisiana's unusual open primary, recently held unconstitutional by the U.S. Supreme Court, benefited incumbents—only one of whom was defeated during the twenty years the system was in place.[36] In Connecticut, a candidate is challenging a state law that requires a candidate for a party's nomination for Congress to receive at least 15 percent of the votes at the nominating convention to qualify for the primary.[37] In Nevada, a voter can check "none of the above" on a ballot. This provision was put in place to siphon off votes from challengers—who would be more likely to receive the nod from disgruntled voters.

Last, but certainly not least, incumbents pass election laws and fund an agency to enforce the laws' restrictions.

FEDERAL ELECTION LAW

Passage of the Federal Election Campaign Act of 1974 was a watershed in the competitiveness of the market for congressional representatives. Prior to the 1974 act, the major restraints were

---

tion.) On a more picayune note, U.S. representative Sue W. Kelly of New York was threatened with being excluded from the ballot because she didn't number the pages of her ballot petitions. (See Greg Pierce, "Technical Error," *Washington Times*, August 6, 1998, p. A6.)

36. See Linda Greenhouse, "High Court Strikes Down Voting Rules in Louisiana," *New York Times*, December 3, 1997, p. A29.

37. See Jonathan Rabinowitz, "Election Law Is Hot Topic in Congressional Primary," *New York Times*, May 19, 1998, p. B6.

prohibitions on contributions from corporations, labor unions, aliens, and U.S. subsidiaries of foreign corporations. The 1974 act made certain changes in presidential campaigns: (a) It provided public funding from a "checkoff" on the individual income tax form, (b) it placed ceilings on spending by those presidential candidates who accept federal funds, and (c) it limited the amount any person could contribute to a presidential campaign. The 1974 act also set restrictions on congressional campaigns: (a) It placed limits on the amounts individuals could contribute, and (b) it placed limits on amounts a candidate for Congress could spend (a provision later held unconstitutional by the Supreme Court in the famous *Buckley*[38] decision).

More than two decades of research has concluded that the major effect of the 1974 reforms was to help incumbents ward off challengers. For example, Peter Aranson and Melvin Hinich demonstrated that the act's limits on contributions and its requirements for disclosure harm challengers more than incumbents.[39] Burton Abrams and Russell Settle found that the Dem-

---

38. See *Buckley v. Valeo*, 424 U.S. 1 (1976). Despite the clear-cut language of *Buckley*, attempts to control spending (as opposed to contributions) persist. A federal appeals court recently invalidated a Cincinnati ordinance placing limits on campaign spending for candidates for the city council. (See Bill Dedman, "Limits on Campaign Spending Are Invalid, Appeals Court Says," *New York Times*, April 28, 1998, p. A14.) The Supreme Court refused to take up the matter on appeal. (See Joan Biskupic, "High Court Refuses Campaign Spending Case, " *Washington Post*, November 17, 1998, p. A2.) A similar law is on the books in Albuquerque. (See Dana Milbank, "Renewed Battle Brewing on Campaign-Spending Caps," *Wall Street Journal*, March 24, 1998, p. A24.) Finally, worth noting is that the European Court of Human Rights recently held that Britain's law limiting the amounts individuals may spend promoting or attacking the views of individual candidates violates fundamental rights. (See Alison Mitchell, "In Europe, Campaign Spending Is a Human Rights Issue," *New York Times*, April 12, 1998, p. WK4.)

39. Peter H. Aranson and Melvin J. Hinich, "Some Aspects of the Political Economy of Election Campaign Contribution Laws," *Public Choice*, 1979, pp. 435–61.

ocrats' support of the 1974 bill was based on their self-interest, inasmuch as Gerald Ford would have beaten Jimmy Carter in the absence of the limits.[40] In a footnote to its decision in the *Buckley* case, the Supreme Court recognized that the Act may advantage incumbents:

> Since an incumbent is subject to these limitations to the same degree as his opponent, the Act, on its face, appears to be even-handed. The appearance of fairness, however, may not reflect political reality. Although some incumbents are defeated in every congressional election, it is axiomatic that an incumbent usually begins the race with significant advantages.[41]

To see how the 1974 reforms help incumbents, reflect for a moment on the maximum amounts individuals may contribute. First, a slew of studies have concluded that the marginal product of spending by challengers is higher than it is for incumbents.[42]

40. Burton A. Abrams and Russell F. Settle, "The Economic Theory of Regulation and Public Financing of Presidential Elections," *Journal of Political Economy*, 1978, pp. 245–57.

41. As quoted in Aranson and Hinich, "Some Aspects," p. 451.

42. See, for example, Aranson and Hinich, "Some Aspects"; Bruce Bender, "An Analysis of Congressional Voting on Legislation Limiting Congressional Expenditures," *Journal of Political Economy*, 1988, pp. 1005–21; Amihai Glazer, "On the Incentives to Establish and Play Political Rent-Seeking Games," *Public Choice*, 1993, pp. 139–48; Gary C. Jacobson, "Money and Votes Reconsidered: Congressional Elections, 1972–1982," *Public Choice*, 1985, pp. 7–62, and "The Effects of Campaign Spending in House Elections: New Evidence for Old Arguments," *American Journal of Political Science*, 1990, pp. 334–62; Christopher Kenny and Michael McBurnett, "A Dynamic Model of the Effect of Campaign Spending on Congressional Vote Choice," *American Journal of Political Science*, 1992, pp. 923–37; John R. Lott, "Does Additional Campaign Spending Really Hurt Incumbents?: The Theoretical Importance of Past Investments in Political Brand Name," *Public Choice*, 1991, pp. 87–92; John L. Mikesell, "A Note on Senatorial Mass Mailing Expenditures and the Quest for Reelection," *Public Choice*, 1987, pp. 257–65; Dennis C. Mueller, *Public Choice II* (New York: Cambridge University Press, 1989), pp. 209–12; K. Filip Palda and Kristian S. Palda, "Ceilings on Campaign Spending: Hy-

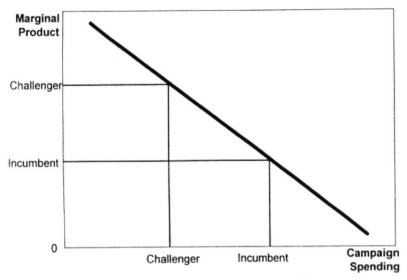

FIGURE 5-1. Marginal Product of Spending—Incumbent versus Challenger

That is, a dollar spent by a challenger will increase her vote margin more than a dollar spent by an incumbent will increase his vote margin. To see why this is so, examine figure 5-1, which assumes that the effect of campaign spending on generating votes (or vote margin) is both positive and declining. It also assumes that the relationship is the same for both the incumbent and for the challenger. Since a challenger usually spends less than the incumbent, the challenger's marginal product (of spending) is higher.

Or, consider figure 5-2, which allows the marginal product curves for the challenger and the incumbent to differ. Everything else equal, a history of having "invested" in advertising and constituent service may make the incumbent's marginal product

pothesis and Partial Test with Canadian Data," *Public Choice*, 1985, pp. 313–31; and Thomas J. Scott, "Do Incumbent Campaign Expenditures Matter?" *Journal of Politics*, 1989, pp. 965–76.

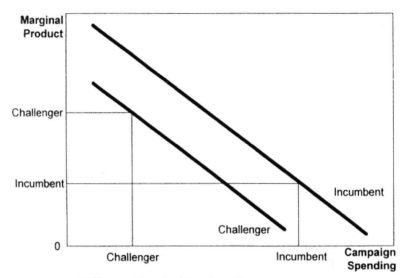

FIGURE 5-2. Different Marginal Product Curves

higher at each level of expenditure than the challenger's.[43] Even so, if the challenger's spending is much less than the incumbent's, the challenger's marginal product may still exceed that of the incumbent. Of course, everything else equal, the fact that incumbents typically have much more contact with constituents than do challengers means that such additional contact, which may be purchased through campaign spending, has lower value in terms of producing votes or vote share. In this case, the incumbent's curve would lie below that of the challenger's, meaning that even if the challenger outspent the incumbent, the former's marginal product could exceed the latter's.[44]

That incumbents tend to spend far more than challengers is a

43. See, especially, Lott, "Does Additional Campaign Spending Really Hurt Incumbents?"

44. As should also be obvious, there is no reason why the two curves might not intersect in one or more places. Also, if the incumbent has "high negatives," the curve may scarcely be positive, consistent with the adage that "nothing can save the incumbent who's lost touch with her constituency."

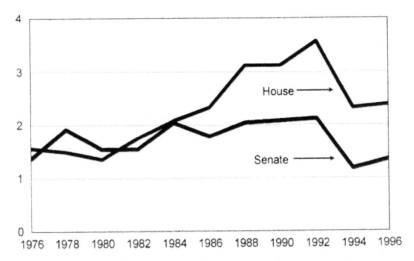

FIGURE 5-3. Incumbent versus Challenger Spending Ratio. (*Source:* Norman J. Ornstein, Thomas E. Mann, and Michael J. Malbin, *Vital Statistics on Congress, 1997–1998* [Washington, D.C.: Congressional Quarterly, 1998], p. 87.)

matter of public record (see figure 5-3). In 1976, incumbents outspent challengers by 56 percent in the House and 37 percent in the Senate; by 1984 House incumbents were outspending challengers by more than 100 percent. Also, the advantages of incumbency in enabling contacts with constituents are clear: (a) polls that show that voters are much more likely to have had personal contact with an incumbent than with that incumbent's challenger,[45] (b) "constituent service" office work undertaken at both the district or state and Washington offices, and (c) the fact that many incumbents spend more on franked mail than their challengers spend on their entire campaigns.

The relative unimportance of money for incumbents and the

45. For example, in 1994, 76 percent of respondents to a poll indicated they had come in contact with the incumbent (personally or through the mail, by means of advertising, et cetera), but only 40 percent had come in contact with the challenger. *Source:* National Election Studies.

key role of money for challengers should not be underestimated. On the basis of a review of the literature and his own empirical analysis, Jeff Milyo concluded:

> The evidence . . . strongly suggests that marginal spending by incumbents has little impact on their electoral success. Even shocks to spending of $100,000 or more produce no discernible impact on incumbent vote shares.[46]

But money is essential to a successful challenge. Money is also important in winning primaries for the purpose of taking on an incumbent. A telling comment on the difficulty faced by challengers due to limits on contributions is provided by columnist and former federal official Linda Chavez:

> When I ran for the U.S. Senate from Maryland in 1986, one of my primary opponents was a wealthy businessman who outspent me by more than 2-to-1, much of it his own money. I couldn't match his personal resources yet had to turn down generous individuals who would have liked to support my candidacy with larger contributions than the law allowed. I remember returning one $10,000 check from a man who had never given to a political candidate before but believed I would make a good senator. He had no agenda—just a dose of political idealism, which the law wouldn't allow him to express as he saw fit.[47]

It should come as no surprise, then, that reforms making it more difficult for both an incumbent and a challenger to raise

46. Jeffrey Milyo, "The Electoral Effects of Campaign Spending in House Elections," Citizens' Research Foundation, University of Southern California, June 1998, p. 27.

47. See Linda Chavez, "Campaign Reform Duplicity," *Washington Times*, April 30, 1998, p. A18. For a similar lament, see James L. Larocca, "Priced Out of Politics," *New York Times*, November 27, 1998, p. A31.

and spend money hurt the challenger more than the incumbent. This is a major reason such restraints are often championed by incumbents.[48] For those who might like to believe that members of Congress promote campaign finance reforms out of a regard for the public interest, consider evidence demonstrating that voting behavior on the campaign finance reforms of 1974 is explained far better by incumbents' interests in being reelected than by any notion of a broader public interest. For example, Bender found that when various spending limits were considered in the House, members' votes were highly correlated with forecasts about the effects such limits would have on their chances for reelection.[49]

DEALING WITH THE REGULATORS

In addition to the effects of the various restraints contained in the act, there is the business of dealing with the Federal Election Commission (FEC), the agency Congress established and charged with the act's enforcement. In dealing with the FEC, incumbents have a natural advantage, both in terms of experience and possible influence. By definition, each incumbent will have gone through at least one campaign dealing with the FEC, and the agency, of course, must come before Congress for its authoriza-

48. Another reason, cited by Mark Crain, Robert Tollison, and Donald Leavens, is that limits on campaign expenditures *increase* the size of government, since those most affected by the limits—such as business firms—tend to oppose efforts by government to redistribute wealth, while others who are relatively unaffected—such as political entrepreneurs for the needy—tend to support such efforts. See W. Mark Crain, Robert D. Tollison, and Donald R. Leavens, "Laissez-faire in Campaign Finance," *Public Choice*, 1988, pp. 201–12.

49. See Bender, "Analysis of Congressional Voting." The spending limits at issue were later declared unconstitutional in *Buckley*.

tion and annual appropriation.[50] Consider what is involved in running for office. Imagine you are a small businesswoman in Iowa or a social worker in South Carolina or a truck driver in Oregon, and you get "fed up" and decide to run for Congress. What then?

Assuming that you know you have to make an initial FEC report (directly to the FEC, in the case of the House, or to the secretary of the Senate) and have to send a copy to the relevant state agency, you must set up a campaign committee, recruit a treasurer, and have that person file on your behalf.[51] In return, your treasurer will receive the following from the FEC: (a) a pamphlet on committee treasurers, (b) a copy of the FEC's latest newsletter, *The Record*, (c) a copy of FEC Disclosure Form 3: Report of Receipts and Disbursements for an Authorized Committee, together with instructions, (d) a list of state offices where copies of all reports must be filed, (e) a reprint of an article describing how to file disclosure reports electronically,[52] (f) a copy of the reporting schedule for the year, (g) a notice about the FEC's fax line, (h) an announcement of upcoming FEC conferences (with no indication whether they are optional or compulsory), (i) a compendium of federal election campaign laws, and (j) a copy of the issue of the *Code of Federal Regulations* dealing with

50. See, for example, Jeanne Cummings, "Louisiana Republican Gives Election Plan a 'No' Vote," *Wall Street Journal*, December 15, 1997, p. A24.

51. Interestingly, the candidate cannot file, only the campaign committee treasurer.

52. The FEC strongly urges candidates to file electronically and even provides software for the purpose. Yet there are notable incompatibilities between the software and what the agency's auditors require. Trying to resolve one such problem (as Treasurer of my spouse's campaign), I was told, "We don't speak to the software people, and they don't speak to us." The FEC has announced a new version of their software, however. See "Electronic Filing Update: FEC Introduces FECFile Version 3.0," *Federal Election Commission Record*, February 1999, pp. 1–2.

federal elections. A total of 618 pages, weighing 1 pound, 12.5 ounces. It's enough to make a candidate reconsider!

That, of course, is only the beginning. Dealing with the FEC can be frustrating and time-consuming—*after* an election as well as before. As an example, consider the letter of inquiry I received following a midyear report submitted more than a year after I had lost a primary election for the U.S. Senate. In relevant part the inquiry reads:

> Your report discloses a . . . loan from the candidate on Line 13(a) of the Detailed Summary Page. It appears that this loan was used to finance expenditures made directly by the candidate (pertinent portion attached). Please note that expenses advanced by the candidate or other committee staff members constitute debts rather than loans; and should be reported in the following manner: the advance should be itemized as a contribution on Schedule A and listed as a memo entry. If, however, the advance was paid in the same reporting period in which it was made, the filing of a Schedule A is not required. When the repayment is made, the transaction should be itemized on a Schedule B supporting Line 17. If the ultimate payee (vendor) requires itemization, it should be listed on Schedule B as a memo entry directly below the entry itemizing the repayment of the advance. Continuous reporting (on Schedule D) of all outstanding debts is required. Please amend your report, if necessary.[53]

The letter was dated September 26, 1997. That very same day, the *New York Times* carried a story entitled "F.E.C. Budget Is No Match for Its Task, Panel Is Told."[54]

53. As was not obvious from the inquiry, the fault lay in my having made a transcription error in my report to the FEC, indicating that a major deposit to the campaign account had been made the day *after* the campaign had written a major check to a vendor.

54. See Francis X. Clines, "F.E.C. Budget Is No Match for Its Task, Panel Is Told," *New York Times*, September 26, 1997, p. A22. The article describes

Or consider how one divines the "right" words to use on the periodic reports when describing the purposes of individual expenditures. In response to a report I made as treasurer of my spouse's campaign came a letter from the Commission's Reports Analysis Division, which reads, in part:

> Commission Regulations define the term "purpose" to mean a brief statement or description of why a disbursement was made. Examples are "dinner expense," "media," salary," "polling," "travel," "party fees," "phone banks," "travel expenses," "travel expense reimbursement" and "catering costs." Unacceptable descriptions include but are not limited to "advance," "election day expense," "expenses," "other expenses," "expense reimbursement," "miscellaneous," "outside services," "get-out-the-vote" and "voter registration." (11 CFR Sect. 104.3(b)(4)) Please amend Schedule B of your report to correct the descriptions which do not meet the requirements of the Regulations.[55]

A request for a *comprehensive* list of acceptable terms was turned down. You just have to guess.

I report these two examples *not* to poke fun at the staff of the FEC, whose job it is to enforce a Byzantine statute. Rather, the purpose is to illustrate a system designed by incumbents to protect incumbents, one that imposes tremendous costs on those least able to cope—challengers.

On a related note, any challenger (or incumbent, for that matter) is liable at any time to have a formal complaint to the FEC lodged against them. This device has become a routine way of orchestrating a "hit" on an opponent—a charge that is leveled but whose veracity is never adjudged by the agency until long

---

FEC testimony before the Senate Committee on Governmental Affairs the previous day.

55. Letter from FEC dated August 18, 1998.

after the election returns are in. Moreover, when the agency investigates the complaint and decides to take no action, it typically responds with the following boilerplate:

> After considering the circumstances of this matter, the Commission exercised its prosecutorial discretion to take no action. ... This case was evaluated objectively relative to other matters on the Commission's docket. In light of the information on the record, the relative significance of the case, and the amount of time that has elapsed, the Commission determined to close its file on the matter.[56]

The problem with this language is that a truly innocent party, should he decide to run again, can be tarred not only with the fact he was the subject of a formal complaint but that after an investigation the commission made no formal finding of innocence.[57]

The burden of dealing with the regulator can be substantial[58] and falls disproportionately on challengers—who frequently

56. This language is taken from a letter from the FEC to my counsel, dated August 29, 1997. It reported the outcome of the FEC's inquiry responding to a complaint lodged by my opponent in my 1996 race for the Republican nomination for the U.S. Senate. To make matters in the case more interesting, my opponent chaired the Senate committee of jurisdiction for the FEC!

In fairness, such cautious legal language is fairly routine among government agencies. When I was chairman of the FTC, similar language was used to notify parties of the closing of an investigation stemming from a complaint lodged by a rival firm.

57. As further evidence of the FEC's having to enforce rules that would seem counterintuitive, I note without further comment O'Keefe and Steelman's observation that the FEC ruled (correctly) that CompuServe's offer to make free websites available to challengers and incumbents alike would violate federal election law. See Eric O'Keefe and Aaron Steelman, "The End of Representation: How Congress Stifles Electoral Competition," CATO Policy Analysis No. 279, 1997, p. 5.

58. A special provision in the law allows candidates for president to set up separate accounts for dealing with legal and accounting issues, and such expenditures do not count toward statutory ceilings.

CHART 5-1. Asymmetry in What Is Allowed—Political Markets versus Commercial Markets

Behavior/Conduct That Is Legal in Political Markets	Analogous Behavior/Conduct in Commercial Markets That Would Constitute Violations of Federal Antitrust or Other Laws
Congress passes laws to "regulate" election process	Members of industry meet and agree to rules under which competition will take place
Congress establishes FEC to interpret and enforce rules	Cartel (above) establishes "enforcement bureau" to make sure rules are followed by all in industry
Congress establishes seniority system and uses it to distribute spoils	Cartel establishes hierarchy and bases rewards on position in hierarchy
Members of Congress agree not to support challengers and to help incumbents	Members of cartel agree to undermine challengers and to support members who are challenged
Members of Congress intimidate (actual and potential) contributors to challengers' campaigns	Members of cartel intimidate customers who show interest in rivals
Members of Congress make false or deceptive claims about themselves or their opponents	Members of cartel make unsubstantiated claims about their products or services or those of their potential rivals
Members of Congress amass and use "war chests" to intimidate would-be (or to defeat actual) challengers	Members of cartel engage in predatory behavior toward potential or actual rivals

must devote a significant portion of the funds they raise to lawyers and accountants just to keep them in compliance with campaign laws and FEC regulations. Whatever the intended goal, the effect of such control is to further insulate incumbents from competition.

MONOPOLY POLITICS

In summary, incumbents rig markets to their own advantage, and so it is correct to conclude that political markets, specifically the markets for choosing representatives to the U.S. Congress, are *monopolistic.*

Incumbents engage in behavior or conduct that would violate laws and result in fines and/or imprisonment if they behaved in an analogous fashion in commercial markets (see chart 5-1). They form a cartel and enforce the cartel's rules. They establish a system of distributing favors that helps incumbents. They agree to come to the aid of one another, in opposition to challengers. Such a pattern, if practiced in commercial markets, would be the subject of rapid legal action, not to mention congressional hearings and extensive commentary in the media. Yet, this all passes for business as usual in political markets. Moreover, as we shall see in the next chapter, serious attention is now being given to proposals that would make political markets even *less* competitive.

CHAPTER SIX

Proposed Reforms

People seem to know, intrinsically, that restraints on trade in commercial markets are unfair and reduce efficiency. Moreover, when they experience poor performance in commercial markets, they are likely to suspect monopoly power and demand redress. But when it comes to political markets, people do not draw the same conclusions—even though in general they don't trust, feel alienated from, and have little regard for politics and politicians. They feel frustrated, but they fail to address the underlying causes of their angst.

Voters put relatively little trust in government, and they trust it less than they did two decades ago. According to the National Election Studies series, trust in government fell from 66 percent in 1966 to 32 percent in 1996.[1] The proportion of the electorate inclined to trust the federal government "most of the time" or "just about always" fell from 65 percent in 1966 to 33 percent in 1996. Whereas in 1966 some 62 percent of the electorate disagreed with the statement, "public officials don't care what

1. Except where noted, the source of all the polling data referenced in this paragraph is the National Election Studies series. This series is available at http://www.umich.edu/nes/nesguide/gd-index.htm.

people think," in 1996 some 62 percent *agreed* with the statement. And where in 1966, by a 60 percent to 34 percent margin the electorate disagreed with the statement "people don't have a say in what government does," in 1996 that feeling had reversed: 56 percent agreed and 34 percent disagreed. In 1996 some 70 percent felt the government is run for a few big interests, up from 33 percent in 1966. A Rasmussen poll found that 77 percent of the population felt that American politicians belong to a political class with its own agenda, whereas only 9 percent believed they represent the people.[2] In 1996, only 7 percent of the electorate gave money to help a campaign, only 5 percent attended a political meeting, and only 2 percent worked for a party or candidate.[3] Moreover, the Internal Revenue Service estimated that only 12.2 percent of individual income tax returns for 1997 included a check mark on the box indicating the filer wanted to send $3 to the presidential election campaign fund—down from the 29 percent peak of about twenty years ago.[4]

There is *some* evidence that people have a suspicion about the fairness, if not the efficiency, of the political market environment. According to another Rasmussen poll, just half of Americans believe that elections are "fair" to voters, and 72 percent agree

2. Polls compiled by the Rasmussen Research Organization and cited in this chapter may be found at http://www.portraitofamerica.com.

3. See also Charles Murray, "Americans Remain Wary of Washington," *Wall Street Journal*, December 23, 1997, p. A14.

4. See "Tax Report," *Wall Street Journal*, April 29, 1998, p. A1. Provocatively, Jeff Clark and Dwight Lee contend that there is an optimal level of trust in government: too much trust, and government will take advantage of the electorate and become undeserving of that trust; too little trust, and government will not be able to attract the type of people and the resources it needs to do its job. See Jeff R. Clark and Dwight R. Lee, "Is Trust in Government Compatible with Trustworthy Government?" in William F. Shughart II, ed., *The Elgar Companion to Public Choice* (Northampton, Mass.: Edward Elgar Publishing, 1999).

with the statement that "in American elections, . . . members of Congress have unfair advantages over people who want to run against them." Moreover, in addition to the polling evidence on alienation, by about two to one people think the federal government is too powerful—which itself is a symptom of monopoly power. Rasmussen also reported that 54 percent of Americans believe that members of Congress who favor disclosure of campaign contributions do so "primarily to learn who is giving to their political opponents" and by a two to one margin think members of Congress might use agencies to harass those who contribute to their opponents. Finally, a Terrance Group poll found that 71 percent of the sample would be less likely to vote for a candidate who voted for a version of campaign finance reform that made it easier for them to be reelected.[5]

Despite this sliver of contrary evidence, the long and the short of it is that people perceive that political markets aren't efficient, but they *aren't* likely to attribute this poor performance to a lack of competitive vigor.[6] Indeed, they often support "reforms" that would make political markets *less* competitive. Thus, if they can be shown why political markets perform poorly and can be convinced that they should be at *least* as adamant in demanding competition in these markets as they are in demanding competition in commercial markets, effective reforms may well emerge.

5. As cited in Peggy Ellis, "10 Big Lies about Campaign Finance Reform," *Washington Times*, October 7, 1997, p. A21. The poll was dated June 1997.

6. Pollster and political strategist Frank Luntz attributed part of the deterioration in the public's trust of political institutions to the revolution in telecommunications. He suggested that when C-Span brought a distant but regal Congress into people's living rooms they were unimpressed. Court TV had a similar effect on the public's confidence in the judiciary. According to Luntz, "the closer people get to the institutions the less they like [them]" (memorandum to author dated March 2, 1998).

"THROW THE BUMS OUT" APPROACH

To the extent people are displeased with the performance of government, their first instinct is to "throw the bums out" and replace them with better people. Yet, substantial turnover in political markets is rare. Since 1950, the proportion of incumbents seeking reelection in the House of Representatives who succeeded fell below 90 percent only five times out of twenty-four, the lowest being 87 percent.[7] Turnover in the Senate has been higher, but since the 1950 election the proportion of incumbents seeking reelection who have succeeded has fallen below two-thirds only four times. Moreover, while during the past three decades reelection rates in the House have remained reasonably stable (averaging between 92 percent and 94 percent), in the Senate they have been rising, averaging 72 percent in the 1970s, 80 percent in the 1980s, and over 90 percent in the 1990s. Perhaps President Reagan's frequent remark, "There's more turnover in the Soviet Presidium than in the U.S. Congress!" was an over-statement—but not by much.

Changes in party control of Congress happen even more rarely. After regaining control of the House of Representatives for one term in the 1952 elections, the Republicans were in the minority until 1994. Republicans in the Senate did only marginally better: After winning a majority for one term in 1952, they relinquished control until winning in 1980, 1982, and 1984 and then being out of power until they won again in 1994.

It is important to stress, of course, that rapid turnover is not a necessary condition for competition in political markets anymore than it is in commercial markets. Indeed, in some industries that

7. The data on reelection rates in this paragraph are taken from Norman J. Ornstein, Thomas E. Mann, and Michael J. Malbin, *Vital Statistics on Congress, 1997–1998* (Washington, D.C.: Congressional Quarterly, Inc., 1998), pp. 61–62.

are fairly competitive there is little vertical mobility. But where barriers to entry exist, as they do in political markets, the lack of turnover is confirming evidence of monopoly power.

Of course, one explanation for low turnover in Congress is that constituents simply *like* their representatives—if you have a history of shopping at Safeway you are not likely to switch to Kroger. Polls do show that voters tend to support their own agents over challengers—feeling more positive toward the incumbent than toward the challenger and by a wide margin (66 percent to 14 percent) approving the incumbent's running for reelection.[8] These results indicating voter preference for the incumbent are understandable, since by definition the agent has been elected at least once before. But surely *some* of this preference reflects the contrived advantage of incumbency: Rather than familiarity's breeding approval, people are responding rationally to the familiar prisoners' dilemma. Although constituents may be critical of Congress in general, they support their agent because, everything else equal, the incumbent can do more for them than could a challenger.[9] This explains why polls frequently show that people are critical of Congress but supportive of their own representative, regardless of party. Thus, they may be enticed to reform the political process, but they will not turn out their agent unilaterally unless given a good reason.

Moreover, there is ample reason to believe that "throwing the bums out" would have little effect on overall performance.[10]

8. National Election Studies series.

9. This is a point consistent with the findings of Scully, mentioned in the previous chapter. See Gerald W. Scully, "Congressional Tenure: Myth and Reality," *Public Choice*, 1995, pp. 203–19. Also, see Einer Elhauge, "What Term Limits Do That Ordinary Voting Cannot," CATO policy analysis no. 328, December 16, 1998, p. 6.

10. Despite the promises made by the new Republican House majority, many believe "the more things change, the more they remain the same." Said Morris Barrett, "If you want more proof that the GOP revolution has not exactly

Certainly, this is the lesson of the research on the "good man" hypothesis in regulatory settings.[11] A new set of decision makers—even a somewhat angelic crowd—would behave in much the same way as the old crowd. What matters much more than the agents' expertise, integrity, and commitment is the institutional environment and the incentives they face.

INSTITUTIONAL REFORMS

People support a range of institutional reforms for Congress (though not all would mean significant improvements in the competitive vigor of the political marketplace). The three institutional reforms receiving the most public attention are: (a) the balanced budget amendment, (b) the line-item veto, and (c) term limits. The effects of each of these three would be to increase the competitiveness of political markets—at least to some degree.

The balanced budget amendment (BBA) has failed to secure the two-thirds vote in each House of Congress necessary to put it before the states for ratification. This failure is not for lack of effort, as in nearly every Congress over the past two decades a serious attempt has been made to accumulate the necessary support. Because the federal deficit, as conventionally measured, has

---

transformed Washington politics, look at the time-honored practice of so-called pork-barrel spending. Congressional lawmakers are pushing pet spending projects as hard as ever, and, while most used to go to the Democrats, it's now the GOP's turn to dish out the financial favors." See R. Morris Barrett, "The Price of Pork," *AllPolitics*, June 9, 1997, available at www.allpolitics.com/1997/gen/resources/pork.

11. This research tests whether an improvement in the performance of regulatory agencies is more likely with a change in key personnel or a change in the institutions and thus the incentives faced by those personnel. The research comes down on the side of the latter. See, for example, George J. Stigler, "The Theory of Economic Regulation," *Bell Journal of Economics and Management Science*, 1971, pp. 3–21; and Sam Peltzman, "Toward a More General Theory of Regulation," *Journal of Law and Economics*, 1976, pp. 211–40.

been eliminated for the time being (thanks to an avalanche of revenue), the BBA's immediate fortunes are fairly bleak.

Eliminating deficit finance as a means of funding government would raise the perceived cost of government and reduce the public's demand for it (at least in times when otherwise the budget would be in the red). This is especially true if the BBA, as in some versions, contained a provision making it harder for Congress and the president to raise taxes (requiring a supermajority vote or even a majority roll call vote of the membership).

Reducing the size of government, or simply restraining its growth, would reduce the economic "rents"—or the various types of favors—representatives would have to spread around. As James Glassman pointed out, "Cut the scope of government, and you'll cut the flow of dollars (or substitutes for dollars, such as donated labor). Nothing else will work. Nothing."[12] Jeff Jacoby opined, "What is corrupting our politics is not money. It is a government grown so powerful and intrusive that virtually anyone with interests to safeguard feels the need to pay protection money to politicians."[13] Fewer appropriations would mean fewer projects for lobbyists to advocate or oppose. Fewer regulatory laws would mean less "rent seeking" on the part of companies and communities—efforts to get the laws and regulations tailored to benefit them and shift costs onto someone else. Moderation in the expansion of entitlement programs in health care and education would reduce advocacy efforts from the medical professions and the education interests.

The reason such a constraint on the size of government would increase the competitiveness of political markets is that presently

12. James K. Glassman, "Campaign Finance Reform Won't Work," *Washington Post*, March 18, 1997, p. A17. See also Glassman, "Let the Cash Flow," *Washington Post*, May 12, 1998, p. A19.

13. Jeff Jacoby, "Reform Fission and Fiction," *Washington Times*, June 12, 1998, p. A20.

much of the interest that stems from larger government gets channeled into political campaigns *disproportionately* on the side of the incumbent. (Recall the data and analysis from the previous chapter.) Constraining the size of government would reduce incumbents' advantage and therefore tend to level the playing field.

The line-item veto suffered a huge setback in 1998 when the Supreme Court ruled the measure unconstitutional because it conflicted with the separation of powers; the only way to overcome this difficulty is to amend the Constitution.[14] Given that it took decades of agitation for the measure before it ever passed Congress by simple majority vote in each House, it would seem safe to conclude that getting two-thirds vote in both Houses to put a line-item veto constitutional amendment before the states is not in the cards. However, such power in the hands of the president would have a minor, but salutary, effect on the competitiveness of federal political markets.

Just as in the case of a BBA, a line-item veto would restrain the growth of government. The effects are not likely to be huge. After all, the amount of pork identified (see table 5-3) is not large, and during the time the line-item veto was in place the amount of appropriations President Clinton vetoed was a minuscule fraction of total spending. But over time, by using the device as a lever to hold down special interest spending, the president could have a small, but significant, restraining effect on the growth of government.[15]

14. *Clinton, President of the United States, et al., v. City of New York et al.*; No. 97-1374; argued April 27, 1998; decided June 25, 1998.

15. The line-item veto enacted into law was a simple binary veto: The President could accept *all* of the appropriated item or eliminate it entirely. Some ten state governors have what is called an "item-reduction veto," which allows the governor to retain the item, eliminate it entirely, *or choose an appropriation amount in between*. Mark Crain and I found the item-reduction veto much more effective than the line-item veto in restraining the growth of spending. See

The term-limit movement at the federal level was delivered a severe blow in 1995 when the Supreme Court ruled that states may not restrict candidates for federal elections.[16] Prior to that decision a number of states had made it difficult, if not impossible, for incumbents to serve more than just a few terms in the U.S. Congress. (The typical limit was six terms in the House and two terms in the Senate.) Understandably, most members of Congress objected strenuously to such laws and breathed a sigh of relief at the Court's ruling. For the same reason, there is little chance that Congress will either amend its own rules to limit terms or approve a constitutional amendment to limit terms without significant persuasion.[17]

But if there were a limit on terms, this would have a significant, positive overall effect on the competitiveness of political markets. First, there would be more open seats (that is, where there is no incumbent). Taking the common "six terms in the House and

---

Mark Crain and James C. Miller III, "Budget Process and Spending Growth," *William and Mary Law Review*, 1990, pp. 1021–46.

16. *U.S. Term Limits, Inc., et al. v. Thornton et al.*; No. 93-1456; argued November 29, 1994; decided May 22, 1995. The case at issue did not involve a state law disqualifying a candidate for Congress who had held the office for more than a given time period, but merely disallowed such a candidate's name from appearing on the ballot. In a sweeping decision the Court ruled that states have no authority "to change, add to, or diminish" the age, citizenship, and residency requirements for congressional service.

17. In the 1994 elections a number candidates promised to limit their terms in office. Several promised to leave after three terms. However, some of those winning in 1994 and winning reelection are having second thoughts. See Jessica Lee, "Some in House have 2nd Thoughts on Term Limits," *USA Today*, December 3, 1998, p. 13A. Also, in the House, there are "voluntary," six-year limits on the terms of full committee chairmen. If these limits are observed, this (1994) reform may have a positive effect on the competitiveness of political markets, since there is evidence that committee service in particular increases incumbent's advantage. (See, for example, Randall S. Kroszner and Thomas Stratmann, "Interest-Group Competition and the Oragnization of Congress: Theory and Evidence from Financial Services' Political Action Committees," *American Economic Review*, 1998, pp. 1163–87.)

two in the Senate" form of the limit, at least one-sixth of the seats in the Senate at each election and the same fraction in the House would be open. Second, the incumbent's advantage would be less. Given a shorter time horizon, vested interests would have less incentive to "invest" in incumbent members and support their campaigns for reelection: They simply wouldn't hold office long enough for the investment to pay off. The incentive incumbents would have to get reelected, whatever the cost, would be less, because the stream of benefits (reelection, possibly in perpetuity) would be smaller since at maximum the story would play out in just a few years. Third, term limits might slow the growth and influence of government and thus reduce the funding advantage of incumbents.[18]

It is important to note here that K. Daniel and J. R. Lott found that term limits in California *reduce* campaign expenditures[19] and that John Carey, Richard Niemi, and Lynda Powell found that term-limited state legislators spend more time on legislation, less on casework, less on fund-raising, and send less pork back to their districts.[20] For those concerned about certain "excesses" in politics, term limits are a one, two (maybe three or more) punch!

The reduction in incumbents' advantage just described would

18. There is empirical evidence that the longer members of Congress serve the more inclined they are to spend. See, for example, James L. Payne, *The Culture of Spending: Why Congress Lives beyond Our Means* (San Francisco: Institute for Contemporary Studies, 1991); James C. Miller III, "Cut Federal Spending—Limit Congressional Terms," *Wall Street Journal*, August 19, 1991, p. A8; and Aaron Steelman, "Term Limits and the Republican Congress: The Case Strengthens," CATO Institute, October 28, 1998.

19. See K. Daniel and J. R. Lott, "Term Limits and Electoral Competitiveness: Evidence from California's State Legislative Races," *Public Choice*, 1997, pp. 165–84.

20. See John M. Carey, Richard G. Niemi, and Lynda W. Powell, "The Effects of Term Limits on State Legislatures," *Legislative Science Quarterly*, 1998, pp. 271–300.

make the challenger more competitive. Knowing that there is now a better chance of the challenger's winning, more money would flow into the challenger's coffers from ordinary citizens and interests alike.[21] While to some extent the reduction in the value of the "prize" might reduce the challenger's ardor for the post, the impact is likely to be small and in any event swamped by the other procompetitive effects just described.

Overall, of the three institutional reforms garnering the most public attention—BBA, line-item veto, and term limits—term limits has the most potential for increasing the competitiveness of political markets.

REVISIONS IN CAMPAIGN FINANCE LAWS

The final major reform garnering substantial public attention is revising the federal campaign finance laws.[22] Proponents of reform point to a variety of "excesses" under the current system and advance proposals designed to eliminate such behavior.[23] To a considerable degree, however, the excesses they identify are

21. After reviewing the literature, Dennis Mueller concludes: "Although interest group giving clearly favors likely winners, both incumbents and challengers receive more contributions, ceteris paribus, when they are involved in close races." See Dennis C. Mueller, *Public Choice II* (New York: Cambridge University Press, 1989), p. 213.

22. For a useful handbook on the federal campaign finance laws, see Anthony Corrado, Thomas E. Mann, Daniel R. Ortiz, Trevor Potter, and Frank J. Sorauf, eds., *Campaign Finance Reform: A Sourcebook* (Washington, D.C.: Brookings Institution, 1997); see also Frank J. Sorauf, *Inside Campaign Finance: Myths and Realities* (New York: Yale University Press, 1992). For a perspective on the campaign finance laws of the various states, see Michael J. Malbin and Thomas L. Gais, *The Day after Reform: Sobering Campaign Finance Lesons from the American States* (New York: Rockefeller Institute Press, 1998).

23. Serious attempts to reform the 1974 act have been made in almost every Congress since 1978. See "Campaign Finance: The Lateral Pass," *New York Times*, August 9, 1998, p. WK-6.

mere symptoms of competition's breaking out.[24] Just as interfirm rivalry and searching by consumers tend to break down or circumvent competitive restraints in commercial markets, candidates and other participants find ways over and around financial restraints in political markets.[25] Illegal contributions and nonreporting of same is one method. But legal means are also available.

Contributions through business and labor political action committees (PACs) are one method. PAC contributions now account for more than one-third of total contributions to campaigns in the House of Representatives and more than one-fifth to campaigns in the Senate (see table 6-1). PACs also fund incumbents far more than challengers (by a ratio of almost five to one); in the 1994–1996 election cycle they split evenly in the House between Democrats and Republicans, whereas in the Senate PAC money went roughly two to one for Republicans (see table 6-1).[26] Finally, the table summarizes contributions of "soft money" to political parties. These are funds that individuals may contribute without limit directly to the parties and that can be used for general support of the party's goals and objectives, but not explicitly to support a party's candidate or to oppose her rival.

Not included in the table is the incidence of "issue ads" in

24. Former (Nixon) White House counsel Leonard Garment was less charitable, if on point, when he noted, "One thing America takes for granted about its politicians is that by hook or by crook they get and spend as much cash as they can to gain office and stay there." See Leonard Garment, "Scandals Past and Present," *New York Times*, March 13, 1997, p. A33.

25. By analogy, during the period before the late 1970s, when U.S. airlines were a regulated cartel, competition broke out in many forms: on-board piano lounges, "sandwich wars" (the agreed-upon sandwich in coach sections of international flights evolved into a full-blown meal), leather seats, greater seat pitch (distance between rows), empty seats (more room and convenience), et cetera.

26. By contrast, during the previous election cycle, before the Republicans took control in both chambers, PAC support split evenly in the House and went for Democrats two to one in the Senate.

TABLE 6-I. Statistics on Campaign Finance

Senate (total), 1991–1992	$216 million
Individuals	66%
PACs	21%
Party	13%
House (total), 1991–1992	$332 million
Individuals	59%
PACs	36%
Party	5%
PAC funding, 1994–1996	
Incumbents	67%
Challengers	15%
Open seats	18%
PAC funding, 1994–1996	
Senate	
Republicans	65%
Democrats	35%
House	
Republicans	50%
Democrats	50%
Soft money, 1995–1996	
Republicans	$138 million
Democrats	$124 million

SOURCE: Federal Election Commission.

targeted markets. This highly controversial exercise of free speech by various nonparty factions (labor unions, advocacy organizations, and other interest groups) is estimated to have totaled between $135 million and $150 million during the 1995–1996 cycle.[27]

27. See Deborah Beck, Paul Taylor, Jeffrey Stanger, and Douglas Rivlin, *Issue Advocacy Advertising During the 1996 Campaign,* report no. 16, Annenberg Public Policy Center, University of Pennsylvania, 1997. It should come as no surprise that candidates and their campaigns are nervous about such advocacy messages, as their effects can be negative as well as positive, and in any event the campaigns lose control. As a recent magazine cover story noted, "After watching what happened in recent special congressional elections in California and New York, candidates and political consultants see the handwriting on the wall and fear this expanding intrusion on candidate campaigns. In fact, their

To put into perspective these efforts to get around strictures on competition in political markets, consider the following. First, the constraints contained in the 1974 act have become more binding over time. The original $1,000 ceiling on personal contributions is equivalent to $3,258 today if adjusted for inflation. Alternatively, $1,000 today purchases what $307 purchased in 1974.[28] And, as incumbents have found additional ways to insulate themselves from competition, it takes more money to mount a credible challenge. Second, some of the exploited "loopholes" were themselves advertised as "solutions" to previous abuses—such as soft money and issue advocacy.[29] Third, finding a solution to the problem involves more hard thinking than evidenced by the oft-repeated admonition that campaign finance reform must be bipartisan, limit spending, and level the playing field[30]—with the second and third criteria, of course, being mutually inconsistent.[31]

---

growing fear of being hit by friendly fire is almost as great as their dread of attack." See Ron Faucheux, "The Indirect Approach: How Advocacy Groups Are Muscling Their Way into the Ring—and What Candidates Are Doing About It," *Campaigns & Elections*, June 1998, pp. 18–24.

28. In a recent decision, a federal appeals court held unconstitutional a Missouri law limiting statewide candidates' contributions to $1,025, saying, "The limits at issue here are so small that they run afoul of the Constitution by unnecessarily restricting protected First Amendment freedoms." See "Asides," *Wall Street Journal*, December 2, 1998, p. A22. On January 25, 1999, the U.S. Supreme Court agreed to review the case (*Shrink Missouri Government PAC vs. Richard Adams et al.*).

29. See, for example, Bradley Smith, "Why Campaign Finance Reform Never Works," *Wall Street Journal*, March 19, 1997, p. A19.

30. See "Pruden on Politics," *Washington Times*, February 4, 1997, p. A4.

31. Part of the problem in addressing campaign finance reform is that federal election laws inhibit informed criticism of the laws themselves. The laws are so complicated that few, other than candidates, have much incentive to learn about them. And candidates—incumbents especially—have little incentive to speak frankly about election laws, because on they whole they benefit by such laws. A parallel with laws enabling the Food and Drug Administration is suggested: Only pharmaceutical firms and attorneys have a sophisticated understanding

Those who seek further restraints on campaign finance seem to be driven, at least in part, by a notion that campaign spending is somehow "out of control" and must be reined in. But let's do a reality check. As discussed in chapter 2, campaign expenditures in political markets are analogous to advertising outlays for products and services in commercial markets. If anything, you would expect campaign (advertising) expenditures in political markets to be more prevalent than in commercial markets because voters have far less incentive to become informed about choices in political markets; those who present themselves as parties or candidates have to make up the difference. In choosing a new automobile, for example, you have a strong incentive to obtain information on makes, models, and prices because such information may be important in your decision *and* your decision will determine the automobile you actually get. In contrast, you have much less incentive to acquire information on parties or candidates since the probability of *your* vote's determining the outcome—the party or candidate you get—is close to nil.[32]

In 1996 the U.S. gross domestic product (GDP) was $7,576 billion, whereas federal spending was $1,560 billion, or 20.6 percent of the total. Advertising in the commercial sector was $175 billion, whereas spending on federal campaigns during the 1995–1996 cycle was approximately $2.2 billion.[33] Let's make

---

of the pertinent laws and regulations, and they have little incentive to speak out about the system's adverse consequences. (I am grateful to Jack Calfee on this point; reference: letter to me dated March 9, 1998.)

32. The same reasoning explains, in part, why voter turnout tends to be far below 100 percent—but this issue is beyond the scope of this work. Suffice it to say, however, that making political markets more competitive would increase turnout. (As noted by the Associated Press, "'98 Voter Turnout Rate Was Lowest in 56 Years," *Washington Post*, February 10, 1999, p. A14.

33. See Jill Abramson, "'96 Campaign Costs Set Record at $2.2 Billion," *New York Times*, November 25, 1997, p. A18 (reporting on a new study by the Center for Responsive Politics).

TABLE 6-2. Response of Candidate Spending and PAC Contributions
to Changes in Federal Outlays and Growth in GDP

Election Period	E: Spending per Candidate versus Federal Budget Outlays* (ratios)	B: PAC Contributions versus GDP** (ratios)
1984 versus 1982	1.2	1.4
1986 versus 1984	1.7	1.8
1988 versus 1986	0.6	1.0
1990 versus 1988	−0.1	0.0
1992 versus 1990	−0.9	2.2
1994 versus 1992	6.2	0.0
1996 versus 1994	−0.4	1.6
1996 versus 1982	0.8	1.1

*E = (% change in spending/candidate)/(% change in federal spending)
**B = (% change in PAC contributions)/(% change in GDP)
SOURCE: Calculations by Parker Normann.

two rough and conservative assumptions: (a) *all* campaign spending is on advertising, and (b) *all* such advertising appears in the
last month of the two-year cycle. Then, if candidates spent at the
same rate during the last month of the campaign (per dollar of
federal spending) as the private sector spent on advertising (per
dollar of total spending in the private sector), campaign expenditures would be around $3.8 billion—which suggests that the
rate of "advertising" in political markets is about half that in
commercial markets.[34] (Another way of saying the same thing is
that even under these highly conservative assumptions, advertising per dollar of "sales" in federal political markets is only about
half as much as advertising per dollar of sales in commercial
markets.)

But is campaign spending growing dramatically? Not according to the calculations by my associate Parker Normann (see table

34. That is, [($175 billion/.794)(.206)]/12 = $3.8 billion.

6-2).[35] During the election cycles from 1982 through 1996, sometimes spending per candidate grew faster than the federal budget (E greater than 1.0), sometimes less fast (E between 0 and 1.0), and sometimes fell below it (E less than 0). PAC contributions showed an uneven record, growing at times greater than GDP and at times less than GDP or even not at all. Comparing the 1982 and 1996 cycles, spending per candidate grew only 80 percent as fast as federal outlays, while PAC contributions grew only 10 percent faster than GDP—hardly a cause for alarm. Yet during the last (105th) session of Congress we were faced with a barrage of demands for campaign finance reform, and the subject promises to be one of the major initiatives of the current (106th) session. Interestingly, most of the public discussion has centered on alleged violations of existing law—topics that dominated the public hearings chaired by Senator Fred Thompson (R.-Tenn.) and Representative Dan Burton (R.-Ind.) during the 105th Congress.[36] But the major reforms go not to tightening the enforcement of existing law but to additional restraints on campaign finance.

A variety of proposals have been advanced to reform campaign finance in federal elections (see charts 6-1 and 6-2). Let's begin with an assessment of the effects of the major bills from the perspective of how they would affect the competitiveness of the market for representatives.

The proposals that have garnered the most support and been the focus of the most attention are the McCain-Feingold bill in

35. Relating candidate spending to federal spending and PAC spending to GDP is somewhat arbitrary, but other denominators (including candidate spending versus GDP and PAC spending versus federal spending) show a similar pattern.

36. Nevertheless, some persist in saying the excesses revealed "loopholes" in the 1974 act (such as the First Amendment?!) since the goals of the act had been subverted. Compare, for example, Jill Abramson, "1996 Campaign Left Finance Laws in Shreds," *New York Times*, November 2, 1997, p. A1.

CHART 6-1. Major Campaign Finance Reform Proposals

Bill Clinton
- Enact McCain-Feingold/Shays-Meehan
- Until then, Democratic National Committee would forgo
  - Soft money if Republican National Committee willing to do likewise (invitation rejected)
  - Contributions from aliens (foreign residents, not U.S. citizens)
  - More than $100,000 from a single donor (since rescinded)
  - Contributions from U.S. subsidiaries of foreign corporations
- Have the Federal Communications Commission (FCC) require broadcasters to offer candidates free air time

McCain-Feingold/Shays-Meehan
- Ban soft money
- Tighten regulation of issue ads (can't use name or likeness of candidate)
- Speed disclosure of contributions and spending during "home stretch"
- Limit out-of-state contributions to 40 percent of total
- Strengthen FEC enforcement
- Limit spending to $600,000 in House contests and to between $1.50 million and $8.25 million in Senate contests
- Bar coordinated party contributions to candidates who don't limit their own personal campaign spending to $50,000
- Make candidates who conform to rules eligible for free or reduced-rate TV time and reduced-rate postage
- Allow union members to receive refunds for dues used for political activity
- Outlaw raising money from foreigners and on government property

Hutchinson-Allen (House leadership–backed alternative to Shays-Meehan)
- Eliminate "soft money" contributions to national, but not state, parties
- Index contribution ceilings for inflation
- Force candidates to file electronically with the FEC
- Require third parties to report information on TV and radio advertisements

Gephardt (House minority leadership)
- Limit nonfederal money that may be contributed to federal campaign or national political party
- Restrict "independent expenditures"
- Prohibit solicitations on behalf of certain nonprofit organizations by candidates and parties
- Require electronic filing of reports to the FEC

CHART 6-2. Other Campaign Finance Reform Proposals

AFL-CIO[a]
- Ban soft money to parties
- Limit campaign spending
- Institute public financing of campaigns
- Limit amount individuals can contribute to candidates, PACs, and parties
- Provide free radio and TV access to candidates, plus reduced postage

Lamar Alexander[b]
- Require full disclosure of all contributions
- End public financing of presidential campaigns
- Stop coerced contributions of union dues for political purposes

Annelise Anderson[c]
- Abolish campaign spending limits
- Abolish campaign contributions limits
- Establish real-time campaign finance reporting requirements

John Anderson[d]
- Until congressional action, parties should
  · Tell candidates they can't accept PAC money, starting with open seats and phasing into seats held by incumbents
  · Insist on spending limits for primaries
- Or parties should take over all fund-raising and dole out funds to "legitimate candidates"

Carter-Ford[e]
- Enhance enforcement of existing campaign finance laws
- Improve disclosure system

John Doolittle[f]
- Eliminate current rules and limits on campaign contributions in exchange for full public disclosure

Pete DuPont[g]
- Repeal limits on contributions
- Report all contributions immediately, electronically to the FEC

Geffroy-Ayres-Bulow[h]
- Put all contributions into a blind fund, which is then turned over to the candidates (identity of contributors is not disclosed)
- Eliminate limits on contributions

Michael McConnell[i]
- Institute a refundable tax credit for contributions to federal candidates—for example, $250 per candidate; $1,000 overall
- Abolish PACs
- Raise limits on individual contributions

CHART 6-2. *(continued)*

Michael McConnell (continued)
- Make contributions above limit anonymous
- Ban contributions for period (for example, six months) *after* election day
- Require candidates to use campaign funds within six months
- Prohibit giving to both sides in an election

Sabato-Simpson[j]
- Require full disclosure of contributions, expenditures, and contacts with regulatory agencies on behalf of constituents
- Eliminate limits on contributions (or raise to $5,000)

O'Keefe and Steelman[k]
- Reduce size of government
- Eliminate ceilings on contributions
- Impose term limits

Ornstein-Malbin-Mann-Corrado-Taylor[l]
- Raise individual contribution ceiling to $2,500 or $3,000
- Encourage small donations with tax credit
- Eliminate soft money for national parties
- Create "broadcast bank," giving candidates and parties free airtime
- Require candidates to file electronically
- Limit tenure of FEC commissioners to one eight-year term

Task Force on Campaign Reform[m]
- Encourage or require broadcasters to grant free airtime to candidates
- Provide partial public funding of campaigns (as with presidential primaries)
- Place reasonable limits on soft money contributions
- Require disclosure of sponsorship of issue advocacy expenditures on campaign-related communications
- Enlarge resources available to the FEC

Washington Post *Editorial Board*[n]
- Institute partial public funding of congressional campaigns in exchange for candidates' adhering to spending limits

Other
- Bruce Ackerman:[o] Institute system of campaign finance vouchers
- Max Frankel:[p] Institute a 100 percent tax on all radio and TV ads and give proceeds to opponent for purpose of making response over same medium
- Horn bill:[q] Allow election officials to check federal records to verify that voters are U.S. citizens
- Shaffer bill:[r] Require a union to obtain prior, written permission before spending a member's dues on political activity

CHART 6-2. *(continued)*

Other (continued)
- Bradley Smith:[s] Repeal Federal Election Campaign Act of 1974
- Paul Taylor:[t] Institute a 50 percent tax on all radio and TV ads and give proceeds to political parties to distribute to their candidates

---

[a] "A.F.L.-C.I.O. Calls for Overhaul of Campaign System 'Awash with Dirty Money,'" *New York Times*, September 23, 1997, p. A25.

[b] Lamar Alexander, "Should Tom Paine Have Filed with the FEC?: The Loss of Common Sense in Campaign Finance Reform," mimeo, Cato Institute, January 21, 1998.

[c] Annelise Anderson, *Political Money: The New Prohibition*, Hoover Institution Press, 1997.

[d] John B. Anderson, "A Quick Fix on Campaign Reform," *New York Times*, February 8, 1997, p. 21.

[e] Jimmy Carter and Gerald Ford, ". . . And the Power of the Ballot," *Washington Post*, October 5, 1995, p. C7.

[f] "Daring Doolittle," *Wall Street Journal*, January 17, 1997, p. A12.

[g] Pete Du Pont, "Price Controls on Democracy," *Wall Street Journal*, September 24, 1997, p. A22.

[h] Fred Hiatt, "Campaign Finance: The Anonymous Donor Plan," *Washington Post*, November 2, 1997, p. C7.

[i] Michael W. McConnell, "A Constitutional Campaign Finance Plan," *Wall Street Journal*, December 11, 1997, p. A22.

[j] Larry J. Sabato and Glenn R. Simpson, "Campaign Reform: A Better Way," *Wall Street Journal*, June 14, 1996, p. A14.

[k] Eric O'Keefe and Aaron Steelman, *The End of Representation: How Congress Stifles Electoral Competition* (Washington, D.C.: Cato Institute, 1997).

[l] Adam Clymer, "Many Proposals but Few Supporters on Campaign Law as Measures Are Languishing," *New York Times*, April 6, 1997, p. A1.

[m] *Campaign Reform: Insights and Evidence* (Princeton, N.J.: Woodrow Wilson School of Public and International Affairs, Princeton University, 1998).

[n] "The GOP Campaign Bill," *Washington Post*, July 18, 1996, p. A26, and "Failed Campaign Finance Reform," *Washington Post*, July 30, 1996, p. A12.

[o] Bruce Ackerman, "Crediting the Voters: A New Beginning for Campaign Finance," *American Prospect*, Spring 1993, pp. 71–80.

[p] Max Frankel, "The Coyote Image," *New York Times Magazine*, March 30, 1997, p. 24.

[q] Helen Dewar and John E. Yang, "Campaign Finance Alternatives," *Washington Post*, September 26, 1997, p. A14.

[r] Ibid.

[s] Bradley A. Smith, "Why Campaign Finance Reform Never Works," *Wall Street Journal*, March 19, 1997, p. A19.

[t] Frankel, ibid.

the Senate and its companion, the Shays-Meehan bill in the House of Representatives. The latter passed in the House in early August 1998, while in early September the former failed to obtain the sixty-vote margin necessary to force a final vote in the Senate.[37] As originally introduced the two bills were slightly different, but the cosponsors remained flexible and the bills coalesced at the end of the session—and therefore they are treated here as one. President Clinton indicated early in the session that he would sign such a measure into law.

Unfortunately, the effects of McCain-Feingold/Shays-Meehan would be to restrict political competition even further. Consider the $600,000 spending limit for House races. As noted by Bradley Smith, in 1996 every incumbent who spent less than $500,000 won versus only 3 percent of challengers who spent that little.[38] Challengers who spent between $500,000 and $1 million won 40 percent of the time, and of those challengers who spent more than $1 million, five of six won. With respect to the proposal's variable limits for Senate races (from $1.50 million to $8.25 million), in 1994 and 1996 every challenger who met the limit lost and every incumbent won.

In other dimensions as well, the proposal would make political markets even *less* competitive. By banning soft money, by treating any ad that uses a candidate's name or likeness as a political expenditure (and therefore subject to more stringent regulation), and by strengthening reporting requirements, giving the FEC more enforcement tools, and increasing penalties, the proposal would further strengthen incumbents over challengers. By barring coordinated expenditures on behalf of candidates who do not limit expenditures from their own pockets to $50,000, the

---

37. See Helen Dewar, "Campaign Finance Bill Buried for Year," *Washington Post*, September 11, 1998.

38. See Bradley Smith, "Why Campaign Finance Reform Never Works."

measure would restrict what recently has been one of the few avenues for successful challenges—the self-financed candidate.[39]

McCain-Feingold/Shays-Meehan contains a provision that would require unions to inform their members that they may apply for a refund of dues devoted to political activities (in keeping with the Supreme Court's decision in *Beck*[40]). But in general, Republicans want more on this front—they want unions to obtain written approval from individual members *before* any dues are spent on political advocacy. Moreover, the Republicans would like to see better policing of voter registration (under the theory that Democrats cast more illegal ballots than Republicans) and higher ceilings on individual and PAC contributions (under the theory that while raising the ceilings might hurt some Republican incumbents, they would advantage Republicans over Democrats even more). Some of these provisions would increase political competition, especially the higher limits on spending, but the Republican incumbents seem more driven by the prospect of gaining competitive advantage over the Democrats than by any interest in increasing the competitiveness of political markets.

Other campaign finance proposals are summarized in chart 6-2. Most of the provisions contained in these proposals overlap those contained in McCain-Feingold/Shays-Meehan. But several provisions are different and worthy of note. First, public financing of campaigns would seem at first blush to be procompetitive inasmuch as it would at least give the challenger a financial base from which to operate. The problem with public funding is that

39. See Larry J. Sabato and Glenn R. Simpson, "Money Talks, Voters Listen," *Wall Street Journal*, December 28, 1994, p. A12. I note here without further comment that the FEC filed and then withdrew a lawsuit against former presidential candidate Steve Forbes, alleging that his columns in *Forbes* constituted an illegal corporate campaign contribution. See "The Election Commission Goes Astray," *New York Times*, September 3, 1998, p. A28; and "Rogue Agency Retreats," *Wall Street Journal*, February 24, 1999, p. A18.

40. *Communications Workers of America v. Beck*, 487 U.S. 735 (1998).

it is usually tied to other requirements—such as matching formulas or limits on spending—that wipe out or even reverse the pro-competitive feature of public funding. Ruth Jones, in analyzing the experiences of seventeen states that between 1972 and 1980 instituted public funding of state-level election campaigns, found that the majority party is generally advantaged by such programs (presumably, one reason for enactment).[41]

Proposals to require broadcasters to provide free or reduced-rate airtime to qualified candidates and requiring the postal service to provide candidates with reduced postage rates would likewise seem to level the playing field—guaranteeing the challenger a modicum of communication with the electorate. These proposals, however, run into serious conflicts with the First Amendment.[42] Similar First Amendment problems are also raised with respect to abolishing PACs, prohibiting contributions to both sides in an election, eliminating soft money, restricting or otherwise regulating media expenditures by advocacy groups, and, most especially, placing limits on total spending.[43] Of these provisions, the abolition of PACs would likely increase the competitiveness of elections since PAC contributions go overwhelmingly to incumbents rather than challengers. Eliminating the practice of giving to both sides in an election (to cover one's bets) would likely reduce competitiveness, for given a choice between

41. See Ruth S. Jones, "State Public Campaign Finance: Implications for Partisan Politics," *American Journal of Political Science*, May 1981, pp. 342–61.

42. See, for example, Donald W. McClellan Jr., "The First Amendment under Siege: The Case against Government Confiscation of Broadcast Air Time for Political Candidates," *Future Insight*, January 1998, pp. 1–17; and Lillian R. BeVier, *Is Free TV for Federal Candidates Constitutional?* (Washington, D.C.: American Enterprise Institute, 1998).

43. See, for example, Lillian R. BeVier, "Campaign Finance 'Reform' Proposals: A First Amendment Analysis," Cato Institute Policy Analysis No. 282, September 4, 1997.

the two, interests are likely to go with the incumbent, not the challenger. But for reasons described earlier, any attempts to limit soft money contributions, issue ads by advocacy groups, and total spending would not only run afoul of the First Amendment, but tilt the playing field more in the direction of the incumbent and therefore reduce the competitiveness of political markets.[44]

On the whole, then, popular initiatives to reform the federal campaign finance laws would make political markets decidedly less competitive, thus compounding the problem that lies behind much of the inefficiencies observed in political markets.

APPENDIX:

A NOTE ON INCUMBENTS' MOTIVES

Why would members of Congress go to such extremes as they have already, much less support even more stringent restraints on competition, given that the system presently works quite effectively from their standpoint? Is it only a matter of preserving their jobs—or is something else involved? Obviously, many members of Congress frankly find it onerous to raise campaign funds. Former Senator Tom Eagleton lamented the loss of Senators John Glenn, Dale Bumpers, and Wendell Ford to retirement and speculated that the reason was that they were simply tired of having to raise money.[45] An alternative explanation, of course, is that

44. Brent Thompson argues that support for campaign finance reform is coming not only from incumbents but from journalists as well: "Constricting free speech rights of private groups and political candidates will increase the influence and power enjoyed by the fourth estate." See Brent Thompson, "Will Campaign Reform Hurt?" *Washington Times*, January 14, 1997, p. A15.

45. See Thomas Eagleton, "Leaving the Senate, Weary of the Chase," *Washington Times*, December 26, 1997, p. A17. Eagleton quotes Bumpers as saying, "The thought of going out with my tin cup was revolting to me," paralleling Ford's observation that "I have no doubt that I could have raised the money, but going around across the country didn't sit well with me." Ibid.

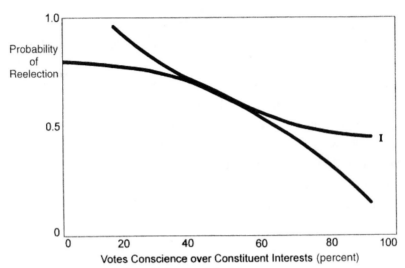

FIGURE 6-1. Incumbent Behavior Model

these long-term incumbents, used to being committee chairmen, saw little chance for the Democrats to reclaim the majority any-time soon.

But still another, at least partial, answer may be found in figure 6-1, which depicts the trade-off members of Congress face between voting their constituents' interests and voting their own consciences.[46] It may also explain to some extent why when mem-

46. On this generally, see Ryan L. Amacher and William J. Boyes, "Cycles in Senatorial Voting Behavior: Implications for the Optimal Frequency of Elections," *Public Choice*, 1978, pp. 5–13; and Rebecca G. Morton, "An Analysis of Legislative Inefficiency and Ideological Behavior," *Public Choice*, 1991, pp. 211–22. Note too the discussion of the principal-agent problem contained in Chapter 4.

Certainly one of the, if not the, most important votes of conscience is over the biennial pay raise. Despite rhetoric to the contrary, the vast majority of members of Congress welcome the prospect of a pay increase and believe they deserve it. Aside from constituent and media pressure, their only reluctance is that higher pay might attract more highly qualified and/or highly motivated challengers. (By law, every two years the president's budget must propose pay adjustments for members of congress, judges, and chief executive officers, based on a study of comparable pay in the private sector; these increases go into effect

bers announce their retirements they sometimes change their behavior.[47]

As shown in the figure, a member of Congress faces a trade-off between maximizing her chances of reelection—by voting her constituents' interests—and voting her own conscience, for which she will pay a price in terms of a lower probability of reelection. (Of course, slavishly voting constituents' interests will not assure reelection, nor will always voting one's conscience assure defeat.) Presumably, a member will choose that degree of "freedom" that maximizes her utility where her indifference curve is tangent to the possibilities frontier. Initiatives to increase the probability of reelection by erecting barriers to competition may be seen, then, as efforts to expand, or "raise," the possibilities frontier. (Ideally, the incumbent would want to face a horizontal possibilities frontier at the 1.0 probability of reelection.) Thus, members of Congress may be going to truly great extremes (erecting legal barriers to challengers, working hard to raise money, intensifying constituent service, et cetera) at least in part in order to purchase the freedom to vote their own consciences rather than their constituents' interests.

---

automatically unless Congress disapproves.)

It is said that House Speaker Jim Wright, who was forced to resign in June 1989, might have survived despite the ethics charge but that what nailed his coffin shut was his mishandling of the congressional pay raise. In the end, members of Congress received enormous heat but no more money.

47. See, for example, Mark A. Zupan, "The Last Period Problem in Politics: Do Congressional Representatives Not Subject to a Reelection Constraint Alter their Voting Behavior?," *Public Choice*, 1990, pp. 167–80. Note, however, that Vanbeek found evidence to the contrary. See James R. Vanbeek, "Does the Decision to Retire Increase the Amount of Political Shirking?" *Public Finance Quarterly*, 1991, pp. 444–56.

CHAPTER SEVEN

Conclusions and Recommendations

What have we learned from this analysis of political markets—and specifically the role of competition? Is there a need for reforms and, if so, what kinds?

SUMMARY AND LESSONS LEARNED

Decisions we make through governments rival in importance those we make in the private sector. Besides establishing and enforcing the legal environment that is meant to protect our constitutional rights, governments engage in myriad activities that affect our material well-being every day. Almost one-third of the gross domestic product (GDP) is "channeled" directly through governments at all levels in the United States (federal, state, and local). When you add the resources that are channeled indirectly (primarily through regulation of all stripes), governments direct or control nearly half of the GDP.

Just as we think of everyday buying and selling activities as taking place in commercial markets, we can think of the decisions we make about and through governments as taking place in political markets. Political markets are remarkably like commercial markets. We "consume with our votes" in political markets just as we "vote with our pocketbooks" in commercial markets. We rely on reputations of parties and endorsements by groups we trust to help guide us in choosing among candidates, just as we rely on the reputations of firms, franchises, and various publications and endorsements to help us get the best deals in commercial markets. Parties and candidates innovate "new ideas" and develop new approaches, just as in the private sector firms engage in substantial research and development of new products and services.

These markets work best when they are open to any and all participants, without any contrived advantages or disadvantages—in other words, where there is *competition.* In political markets as well as commercial markets, participants have an incentive to monopolize. There is a long history in our country of antagonism toward monopoly power in commercial markets. The antitrust laws were specifically designed, first, to keep monopoly from happening in the first place and, second, to break up monopolies that get through this initial screen. Elaborate mechanisms are in place today to police monopoly in commercial markets, and some of the most ardent supporters of such laws are members of Congress.

Likewise, in political markets there is a strong incentive to monopolize. The payoff is less obvious because the bottom line is not profits in the usual sense. Rather, the goals of monopolizing are power (having one's way about policy), adulation, feeling important, being free from criticism, and so forth. Just as in commercial markets, monopoly in political markets shortchanges the relevant consumers—that is, voters. It allows representatives to pursue their own interests rather than the interests of their constituents. Just as in commercial markets, victims of monopoly pay higher prices and get less in return.

Political markets differ from commercial markets in important ways, however. First, whereas in commercial markets we make decisions *individually*, in political markets we make them *collectively*. Your purchase of a Swatch watch doesn't bother your friend who prefers the Timex—you both get your choice. But if the decision about watches were made collectively—by your Rotary Club, for example—unless the Swatch were chosen you wouldn't be happy, and unless the Timex were chosen your friend wouldn't be happy. Thus, in political markets, opportunities for tailoring outcomes to suit the preferences of all individual voters (consumers) are more limited than in commercial markets. But what about the collective decision rule? Does the ubiquitous majority rule lead to an outcome that somehow satisfies more or makes as few as possible unhappy with the outcome or both?

That question has been the subject of extensive research over the past several decades, and the answer comes down to a qualified yes. Ideally, you would want a unanimity rule since then no change would make one voter better off without making some other voter worse off—analogous to the efficiency test known as Pareto optimality in commercial markets.[1] But achieving such ultimate consensus is not practical for most collective decisions. Consequently, we adopt less rigid requirements—usually a simple majority. As it turns out, under majority rule the winner of a political contest will reflect the view of the median voter where the issue can be seen as one-dimensional (liberal versus conservative, guns versus butter, et cetera) and will reflect the views of the *mean* voter where the issue has multiple dimensions. For practical purposes, one may conclude that in either case majority rule leads to a relatively efficient outcome in political markets.

1. As a step in that direction, Jim Buchanan and Roger Congleton have recommended that collective decisions comport with a generality principle analogous to the principle of equal justice under law. See James M. Buchanan and Roger D. Congleton, *Politics by Principle, Not Interest: Toward a Nondiscriminatory Democracy* (Cambridge: Cambridge University Press, 1998).

That is, in a rough and ready sort of way, majority rule leads to outcomes where the satisfaction of voters is maximized and the dissatisfaction is minimized.

Political markets also differ from commercial markets inasmuch as voters are usually "stuck" for a period of time with the representatives they choose at the ballot box, whereas in commercial markets consumers who become dissatisfied can change from one seller to another instantaneously. This problem is magnified by the "distance" between voter and representative and the discretion the representative has to follow his own interests rather than the interests of his constituents.

In view of these "imperfections" in political markets, how efficient are they in practice? There are two views. One view holds that political markets approximate the efficiency one could expect from any market, including ordinary commercial markets. Voters find ways around each "imperfection," rewarding representatives for doing the "right thing" and penalizing them for doing the "wrong thing." The other view is that the discretion afforded representatives, combined with the incentives they have to utilize it, means that actual outcomes seldom reflect accurately the views of the median (or mean) voter. That view points to imperfections in the decision rules of Congress, for example, which give each unit (district or state) an incentive to obtain as much from government as possible while having others pay the bill. The ensuing behavior by representatives leads to governments that are excessive in size and cater unduly to special interests.

A resolution of these views appears possible, however. To a considerable degree the difference between the two hinges on the presumed degree of competition in political markets. The former view *assumes* a competitive electoral process. The contrary view *assumes* a lack of competition. If there were more competition, representatives would have less discretion to act in ways contrary to the views of their constituents. If there were more competition, the market imperfections that lead people to underestimate the true costs of government—and therefore to demand too much of it—would be ameliorated or even eliminated. In short, under either view, competition is key to improving the efficiency of political markets.

It is hard to dispute the conclusion that "monopoly power" now characterizes political markets, especially the market for choosing representatives to the federal legislature. Incumbents have enormous, contrived advantages over challengers. It's hardly a level playing field. First are the assets of office—franked mail, caseworkers in the field, and an ability to deliver "pork" and other goodies back to the district or state. Members are also in a position to intimidate potential contributors—coercing them to contribute to them and not to contribute to any challenger. In addition, members of Congress collude with one another and with officials of their state governments to rig the electoral rules in their favor.

Incumbents also have established federal laws that effectively insulate them from competition. In particular, limits on the amounts individuals and political action committees (PACs) may contribute restrict the funds candidates may raise. Extensive research has shown that such limits harm challengers far more than incumbents. Moreover, research has shown that voting on such limits appears to have been motivated by the desire of representatives to limit the effectiveness of challengers. Incumbents also have an advantage in dealing with the major campaign regulator, the Federal Election Commission (FEC). The reporting and other requirements faced by candidates are intimidating, to say the least, and someone new to the process is naturally disadvantaged in comparison with someone who, by definition, has coped with the process successfully on at least one prior occasion and who likely has the wherewithal (leftover campaign funds) to hire the accountants and lawyers needed to meet the agency's requirements and to respond to its demands.

There is a fundamental asymmetry in the public's attitude toward monopoly in commercial markets and monopoly in political markets. If the titans of business were to meet without government sanction and establish rules to make it harder for new entrants to come in and serve the needs of consumers, they would be slapped with restraining orders, public inquiries, and criminal penalties in nothing flat. If business firms intimidated customers to the extent of their not patronizing new, competitive firms, the reaction of the antitrust enforcement agencies would be swift and sure. If some firm in the private sector were to make unsubstantiated claims about a rival's product or service, or false claims about the virtues of its own product or service, severe penalties would ensue. The fact is that analogous behavior in political markets goes unpunished—and indeed, to a major extent, unrecognized. Part of the problem is that the press and the public are not attuned to recognizing such behavior for what it is—monopoly. But the major part of the problem is that the people making the rules of the game are the very ones who benefit from having the rules advantage incumbents and disadvantage challengers.

Several major proposals have been advanced that would affect the competitiveness of political markets. Unfortunately, the ones that would increase their competitiveness stand little chance of enactment. Still more unfortunately, the proposal receiving the most public attention, and most likely to be enacted, would actually make matters worse. Both the balanced budget amendment (BBA) and the line-item veto would restrain the growth of government, limit the economic "rents" that representatives are able to pass around, and therefore limit the funding differential between incumbents and challengers (special interests give to incumbents overwhelmingly). However, the BBA was not able to garner the needed two-thirds majorities in both Houses while deficits were large and growing, and in today's climate of (technical) surpluses it is even less likely that a BBA will be approved and offered to the states for ratification. The line-item veto got a trial run last year, as it survived review by the district court and the court of appeals, but it was overturned by the Supreme Court, which ruled that the measure conflicted with the separation of powers between Congress and the president. Term limits would have a significant, positive effect on the competitiveness of political markets by increasing dramatically the number of open seats in each election and by changing the incentives of both incumbents and challengers. The movement for term limits was experiencing considerable success, as many individual states were limiting the terms of *their* representatives to the federal legislature. But this strategy was terminated by the Supreme Court in 1995, when it ruled that states cannot place eligibility requirements on candidates for federal office. Given that no initiative for a constitutional limit on terms has ever garnered anywhere near the necessary two-thirds majorities in either House, and given that such a limit would be so contrary to the interests of the very people making the decision, it is unlikely that incumbents will approve such an amendment without substantial pressure to do so.

The final major initiative—campaign finance reform—is the one that seems most likely to be enacted. Unfortunately, its effect would be to restrict competition even further. Although well intentioned, at least by its sponsors and some of its supporters, the current legislative vehicle, McCain-Feingold/Shays-Meehan, would severely disadvantage challengers vis-à-vis incumbents. By constraining contributions—and thus fund-raising—even further, the initiative would increase the disparity between the resources available to incumbents and those available to challengers. By strengthening FEC enforcement powers and narrowing the discretion of groups to support candidates, the bill would further tilt the playing field toward the incumbent. By making it more difficult for a candidate to finance her own campaign, the bill would limit this means of mounting a successful challenge.

Other campaign finance proposals have provisions that could increase competition in political markets, but several—such as public financing of campaigns in exchange for limits on spending—would have the reverse effect. Also, although some—such as requiring broadcasters to provide free or reduced-rate airtime to political candidates—might reduce the disparity in resources available to incumbents versus challengers, they run into severe First Amendment difficulties. This is particularly true of proposals to restrict campaign spending overall, to eliminate PACs, and to circumscribe issue ads by advocacy groups.

The unnerving fact is that no major proposals on the horizon would address the core problem of political markets, namely, a lack of competition. Indeed, the challenge today is to prevent Congress and the president from enacting "reforms" that just make matters worse.

NEEDED REFORMS AND PLAN OF ACTION

It is easy to see from the analysis what *not* to do if the objective is to increase the competitiveness of political markets: Do *not* do anything to increase the advantages of incumbents. Nor should we try and cut off ways in which competition is breaking out. What we need is a direct attack on the numerous anticompetitive features of political markets, not a plinking away at symptoms.

Because few plans to reform government are adopted in their entirety, it is best to include some redundancy in any set of recommendations. Although the set of reforms outlined below are designed to improve the competitiveness of the market for choosing representatives to Congress, they could be adapted to other political markets. And though not all are necessary to achieve a significant increase in competitiveness, omission of one or more could limit the improvement in efficiency.

Let us start with contrived advantages of incumbency and then move on to address broader impediments to competition.

1. *Limit the perquisites of office.* We should limit "perks" to those essential for members of Congress to be effective representatives—and therefore limit this form of advantage that incumbents hold over challengers:

a. Eliminate unrequested franked mail. Each member of Congress has an obligation to respond to specific requests from constituents for information or even, on occasion, for help with problems they have dealing with the bureaucracy. The cost of such correspondence, including postage, is a legitimate expense of office. But some members of Congress make mass, unrequested ("postal patron") mailings to constituents that are little more than campaign literature in disguise. Such campaigning at taxpayer expense—a benefit not available to challengers—should be terminated. Although recent reforms in the rules limit representatives' budgets for franked mail and forbid mass mailings within sixty days of an election,[2] they do not go far enough. The prohibition on (taxpayer-funded) unrequested mail should be absolute, should apply to the Senate as well as to the House, and should be made part of permanent law, not merely the rules of the respective Houses.

b. End the free use of Capitol TV and radio studios. Most interviews and "reports" to the district or state that emanate from this facility are little more than disguised campaign messages. The costs should be borne not by taxpayers but by the incum-

2. See United States House of Representatives, 106th Congress, Rule XXV, para. 8; and United States Senate, Standing Rule 40, para. 1.

bent's campaign committee. (Challengers have no such taxpayer-funded benefit.)

c. Cut the size of congressional staffs. Congressional staffs have grown substantially over the past two decades, with the increment being devoted to "constituent service," a substantial portion of which involves dealing directly with agencies. Such taxpayer-funded casework bestows an enormous advantage on incumbents. Congress should reduce the *need* for such service by making laws more explicit and holding agencies more accountable. To the extent such service is still necessary, Congress should establish and fund a program of regional "ombudsmen" as part of the executive branch.

Other limits on perquisites are easier to agree with in principle than in application. Nevertheless, significant progress can and should be made on these more subjective, less easily measured, goals:

d. Eliminate "pork" in the budget. For the sponsor, the project at issue may be fundamental to the national defense. But as the Supreme Court said of pornography, "you know it when you see it." The definition of pork adopted by Citizens Against Government Waste (see table 5-3) would be a good place to start. Elimination of pork would help level the playing field since challengers have no access to this taxpayer-funded benefit.

e. Control the proliferation of legislation. The vast majority of bills introduced in Congress each year get no more attention than the ticking of a watch *except* to the extent the sponsoring members of Congress can use the bill's introduction as a means of convincing his constituents that he has engaged in a major undertaking and is a real player. More important, new laws are often designed to create additional opportunities for members of Congress to "serve" their constituents. Limiting the number of legislative initiatives and making new laws more specific would curtail sham claims of effectiveness, reduce the additional "rents" that directly advantage incumbents with voters, and narrow the funding margin incumbents maintain over challengers.

f. Limit discretion of regulatory agencies. At present, members of Congress enact vaguely worded regulatory laws, take credit for having addressed an important issue, then delight in the additional casework generated by agencies that use their discretion in ways constituents find arbitrary. Limiting agency discretion would reduce the demand for taxpayer-funded incumbent advantages and their funding edge over challengers.

g. Scrap the tax code and start over. No other set of laws gives rise to more rent-seeking, favor-buying, and incumbent-protection advantages than the Internal Revenue Code, as lobbyists from far and wide wrangle to obtain special favors for clients. Starting over with a simple, flat tax on either income or consumption would reduce greatly the contrived advantage now afforded incumbents.[3]

2. Reform the federal election laws. Formal rules establishing the parameters within which competition for representatives to the federal legislature takes place should be reformed to increase transparency, fairness, accountability, and competitive vigor:

a. Eliminate ceilings on campaign contributions. As discussed in chapter 5, the evidence is clear that the major effect of ceilings on campaign contributions is to benefit incumbents over

3. The flat tax on income is championed by Congressman Dick Armey among others. (See, for example, Dick Armey, *The Flat Tax* [New York: Fawcett Book Group, 1996].) The flat tax on consumption is championed by Congressmen Bill Archer and Billy Tauzin and several of their colleagues. (See, for example, Billy Tauzin, *National Retail Sales Tax: April 15 Just Another Day* [Baton Rouge, La.: Claitors Publishing Division, 1998].) The seminal work on the flat tax (on income) is Robert E. Hall and Alvin Rabushka, *The Flat Tax*, 2d ed. (Stanford: Hoover Institution Press, 1995).

challengers. Also, as we saw in the last chapter, the amount of money involved in political campaigns, at least judged by standards of the private sector (advertising), is not excessive. Moreover, placing limits on the amounts individuals and PACs can contribute only increases pressure for contributors and candidates to find ways around such restraints. Eliminating ceilings on contributions would not only end this form of contrived advantage for incumbents, but would go far in eliminating the "abuses" that give rise to some of the current demands for misguided campaign finance reforms—such as eliminating "soft money," "coordinated expenditures," and issue advertising by advocacy groups.[4]

    b. Require complete *disclosure of* all *contributions.*   Federal law currently requires that in-kind contributions be reported to the FEC. But one has the notion that this requirement is honored more in the breach than as a matter of course. Exceptions should be made for minor contributions, such as the oil and gas it takes to drive over to the campaign office to volunteer. But when a major organization (such as a union or business enterprise) "volunteers" considerable resources to aid a campaign, those resources should be reported just as quickly and as accurately as financial contributions. The whole purpose of disclosure is so that voters will know just who is supporting the candidates and

---

    4. Not only does opposition to spending limits draw support from a variety of quarters (see Katherine Q. Seelye, "Army of Strange Bedfellows Battles Spending Limits," *New York Times*, March 15, 1998, p. A10 [citing opposition by the American Civil Liberties Union, the National Association of Broadcasters, and the Christian Coalition]), but opposition to limits on *contributions* does as well (compare, for example, letter from Ira Glasser, executive director of the American Civil Liberties Union, "ACLU Opposes Limits on Campaign Finance," *Wall Street Journal*, May 13, 1998, p. A23; and opposition by Senator Mitch McConnell, leader of the antireform forces in the Senate [see Mitch McConnell, "Reform Violates Free Speech," *USA Today*, December 1, 1998, p. 14A]).

to whom the candidates might be indebted after the election. Such in-kind donations are no less appreciated (and "indebted") than the financial kind.

c. Tighten laws and enforcement against intimidation. Because of the extraordinary potential for abuse of power as well as for the effects on the competitiveness of political markets, the laws against intimidation, and particularly the enforcement of those laws, should be tightened so as to prevent representatives from "shaking down" contributors.

d. Eliminate "war chests." Because incumbents effectively use war chests to intimidate challengers, all candidates should be required to dissipate campaign surpluses within a short time after the election (for example, within six months, as suggested by Michael McConnell—see chart 6-2). The uses of such funds should be circumscribed so that they do not inure to the benefit of the candidate (for example, no charitable contributions to institutions in the district or state, and no contributions to other political candidates or organizations that might reciprocate either in kind or in cash).

e. Streamline standards and enforcement by the FEC. With no limits on contributions, some of the FEC's work, and the requirements faced by candidates, would disappear. This would tend to level the playing field between incumbents and challengers. But more should be done. The maximum an individual may contribute to a campaign (in any given year) without requiring detailed reporting to the FEC should be raised from $200 (unchanged since 1974) to $1,000. This would reduce reporting enormously, without much loss of relevant detail. Also, the FEC should improve its electronic filing software and simplify its reporting standards and requirements.

f. Encourage the courts to review state redistricting plans. Redistricting for the purpose of affecting the partisan makeup of state delegations is a legal and well-understood (though arguably improper) use of state power. But the real gerrymandering that takes place is over ways to protect incumbents. Courts should be encouraged to review state redistricting plans that come before them for evidence of "incumbent protection" and find them unacceptable on grounds of unequal treatment (of candidates) under the Constitution.

g. Task the attorney general to test preferential state laws. The U.S. attorney general should be tasked to test the constitutionality of all state election laws that are suspected of granting one type of candidate or party preference or advantage over another. Examples include unduly burdensome requirements for a third (or fourth) party to get on the ballot (while the major parties qualify automatically); unduly high filing fees (which incumbents are more likely to afford than challengers); and laws, such as Virginia's, that, under certain circumstances, give an incumbent the right to choose the method of party nomination.

3. Revise institutions. The most lasting reforms are those that change the basic institutions and the incentives facing the participants:

a. Disestablish the seniority system as a means for wielding power. Having more influence because of wisdom accumulated through experience is perfectly legitimate. But aspects of seniority that artificially determine the power at a member's command should be modified so that incumbents do not automatically have a superior claim to resources and effectiveness.[5]

b. Rotate memberships, as well as chairmanships, of committees. The House of Representatives has taken a step to limit the term of the chairmanships of full committees, but this is not enough. The rule should apply to the Senate as well and should

---

5. The incentives established by seniority also increase longevity and discourage dissent among new members.

be made part of permanent law. Also, rotating memberships on committees would lessen the incentive of interests dependent on specific committees to "invest" in particular members. This would reduce the contrived funding advantage of incumbents over challengers.

c. Impose term limits. More than anything else, the imposition of term limits would increase the competitiveness of political markets. (See discussion in previous chapter.) Obviously, overcoming the self-interest of members of Congress to get a constitutional amendment before the states for ratification will not be easy. But there would be significant improvements in efficiency from such an initiative.

Finally, let us explore the possibilities of improving the competitiveness and efficiency of collective decision making through application of the digital revolution.

Why is it that we have *representative* democracy as opposed to *direct* democracy anyway?[6] Part of the answer is that it is an artifact of history. When the country was established we chose one of our neighbors to get on a horse and ride to the state capital or to the national capital to represent us. Obviously, it was simply not feasible for us to participate directly in the decision making ourselves. Another reason for representation is that even if it were feasible to participate directly, we just don't have the time. Still another reason is that even if we had the time we might prefer to trust someone else's judgment on matters with which we don't feel comfortable.[7]

6. Interestingly, Rexford Santerre found that people are willing to pay a premium to live in communities with direct democracy. See Rexford E. Santerre, "Representative versus Direct Democracy: A Tiebout Test of Relative Performance," *Public Choice*, 1986, pp. 55–63.

7. Direct democracy has its critics. For example, Eli Noam has argued that direct democracy leads to inefficient outcomes because there is no opportunity

How might the digital revolution be applied to all this? First, a degree of participation that years ago was unthinkable is not exceptional today and will be quite common tomorrow—satellite conferencing, interactive web pages, and the like. As I proposed three decades ago,[8] the Constitution might be amended to accommodate *direct* participation of voters in the affairs of state, bypassing their elected representative when conditions or interest warranted, or giving a proxy to their own preferred representative. Failing that, the digital revolution could solve one of the greatest imperfections in political markets, which is that once a representative is selected voters have few realistic alternatives to waiting out their terms should their representative fail to perform.[9] In the digital age, it should be possible for voters to recall representatives almost costlessly and instantaneously, just as

---

for vote trading. See Eli M. Noam, "The Efficiency of Direct Democracy," *Journal of Political Economy*, 1980, pp. 803–10.

8. See James C. Miller III, "A Program for Direct and Proxy Voting in the Legislative Process," *Public Choice*, 1969, pp. 107–13. In that piece, I suggested that people make political decisions by means of networked personal computers, with the computers verifying the users' identification. Such a technology now exists—networking (including the Internet), plus fingerprint ID (see "PC Fingerprint ID," *Popular Mechanics*, February 1998, p. 30). Also, the state of Texas has arranged for astronauts who are citizens of the state to vote encrypted ballots via laptops from space. (See Sam Howe Verhovek, "Giant Leap for the Space Crowd: Voting," *New York Times*, August 26, 1997, p. A10.) But as pointed out to me by Miller Baker, such a system undercuts the secret ballot, since, as in the case of ordinary absentee ballots and Oregon's new system of mail-in ballots, the voter's choices may be checked by another party (e-mail to me dated November 19, 1998).

9. It is interesting to reflect on the views of Chinese dissident Wei Jingsheng, who was recently released from prison in order to come to the United States for medical treatment: "What is true democracy? It means the right of the people to choose their own representatives to work according to their will and in their interest. Only this can be called democracy. *Furthermore, the people must also have the power to replace their representatives any time so that these representatives cannot go on deceiving others in the name of the people*" (emphasis added). See "The Democratic Banner Cannot Be Obscured," *Wall Street Journal*, November 18, 1997, p. A23.

they, as consumers, can change sellers costlessly and instantaneously if they are displeased with the products or services they receive.[10]

In conclusion, political markets are far less responsive to the will of the people than they could be—and the problem is monopoly power. To eliminate this monopoly power, significant steps must be taken to eliminate the contrived advantages enjoyed by incumbents, and other steps must be taken to broaden opportunities for challengers and ordinary voters to participate. That's the opportunity. The danger, though, is that, partly from good intentions, partly from bad, Congress and the president seem poised to pass campaign finance reforms that will make matters worse. Which will it be? Will we seize the opportunity to make politics more efficient and more responsive—or will we treat the symptoms of a malfunctioning market by making the patient worse?

10. The digital revolution, and the associated revolution in communications, may have other effects. For example, Douglas Hart and Michael Munger found that the incumbent's advantage is inversely related to the distance between the district (or state) and the nation's capital and suggested that improvements in communications and transportation will *increase* incumbents' advantage. See Douglas B. Hart and Michael C. Munger, "Declining Electoral Competitiveness in the House of Representatives: The Differential Impact of Improved Transportation Technology," *Public Choice*, 1989, pp. 217–28.

INDEX

Abrams, Burton, 89
Ackerman, Bruce, 122
advertising: content of, 19; FTC
  regulation over, 26; function of,
  37; political issue-attack vs. image-
  attack, 61; restricting free political,
  139–40; restrictions under
  antitrust laws on, 59; sale vs.
  market shares and, 19; spending of
  commercial vs. political, 117–18
AFL-CIO campaign finance reform
  proposal, 121
Alexander, Lamar, 121
Amacher, Ryan, 55
American Conservative Union, 36
American Federation of State,
  County, and Municipal
  Employees, 36
Americans for Democratic Action,
  36
Anagnoson, Theodore, 82
Anderson, Annelise, 121
Anderson, John, 121
anticompetitive mergers, 25
antitrust laws: election laws
  compared to, 42–45; as linchpin
  of capitalism, 27; overview of, 24–
  27; rent-seeking behavior and, 29–

30; restrictions on advertising by,
  59; used to limit competition, 30–
  31, 132. *See also* economic
  regulations; U.S. regulatory
  agencies
Aranson, Peter, 89
AT&T antitrust settlement of 1981,
  28

balanced budget amendment (BBA),
  108–10, 113, 136–37
ballot measures: Colorado's rules
  for, 57–58; used to override
  decisions, 56–57
Becker, Gary, 66
Bennett, Randall, 81
Bickers, Kenneth, 80
Black, Duncan, 49
Box-Steffensmeier, Janet, 83
Boyes, William, 55
Brumberg, Bruce, 77–78
Buchanan, James, 49, 71
Buckley decision, 89, 90
Bumpers, Dale, 127
Burton, Dan, 119

CAB (Civil Aeronautics Board), 28
campaign contributions: abuses

"Here at last is a thoughtful, scholarly, and yet accessible volume that explains the effect of campaign finance reform on competition in politics. The book could not be more timely, given the current debate on campaign reform, and this reasoned thesis will inform both the players in the debate as well as citizens who care about the future of the system."
> —Larry Sabato, political scientist,
> University of Virginia, and
> coauthor, *Dirty Little Secrets*

"Splendidly, if depressingly, right. Term limits would be best, but fending off McCain-Feingold is not bad."
> —George Will, *Washington Post* columnist
> and ABC-TV commentator

"Jim Miller reminds us that we've failed to appreciate the role of competition in politics. His analysis is perceptive and his conclusions on point."
> —Newt Gingrich, former Speaker,
> U.S. House of Representatives

"Jim's application of public choice theory to politics is compelling. In Jim's fundamental conclusion—the need to increase political competition among candidates, ideas, and factions—can be heard echoes of those great thinkers who span the political divide: Oliver Wendell Holmes and James Madison."
> —Charles Mannatt, former Chairman,
> Democratic National Committee

"Jim Miller knows more about the theory behind incumbent advantage than anyone in America. Anyone who cares about elections and the democratic process owes it to themselves and to America to read this book."
> —Frank Luntz, pollster for Ross Perot
> and other candidates

JIM MILLER is a fellow at the Hoover Institution and is John M. Olin Distinguished Fellow at Citizens for a Sound Economy Foundation as well as at the Center for Study of Public Choice at George Mason University. Throughout his distinguished career he has held a number of key positions in government, including chairman of the Federal Trade Commission (1981–1985), director of the U.S. Office of Management and Budget, member of President Reagan's cabinet, and member of the National Security Council (1985–1988). He has also served on the boards of directors of several companies and is currently on the boards of Atlantic Coast Airlines (United Express) and Washington Mutual Investors Fund.

Miller's experience in electoral politics includes races for the Virginia Republican U.S. Senate nomination in 1994 (he lost a close race to Oliver North) and 1996 (he lost to incumbent John Warner). In 1998 he was treasurer of his wife's campaign to represent Virginia's 8th Congressional District, in which she won the primary but lost the general election.

Frequently called on to comment on public issues, Miller has appeared on the *Today Show*, *CBS Morning News*, *Good Morning America*, *Meet the Press*, *This Week*, *Crossfire*, and *Wall Street Week*. His opinion pieces have been published in major newspapers across the country, including the *New York Times*, the *Washington Post*, the *Wall Street Journal*, and *USA Today*.

He and his wife, Demaris, currently reside in McLean, Virginia, and on Flattop Mountain in Greene County, Virginia.

premiums over thirty years, invested those profits, and ultimately, never had to pay a death benefit.

OPPORTUNITY COST BEYOND 30-YEAR TERM INSURANCE

Present value: $58,661

Interest rate: 6 percent

Number of years: 20

FUTURE VALUE: $188,134

The loss of the death benefit at death is the largest cost to the individual. In our example above, that was an additional $1,000,000 on top of the $188,134 for a total of $1,188,134 of lost wealth to a spouse, loved ones, or charity. Upon full analysis, term life insurance is by far the most expensive life insurance anyone could ever own.

The financial entertainers tell us to buy term and invest the difference. After all, term insurance is cheap. People can take the amount they save (the difference in premium costs between a term and permanent insurance policy) and invest it in the stock market. At first glance, this strategy seems to make sense, but from a macro-economic standpoint it is financially devastating. As David Babbel, professor at the Wharton School of the University of Pennsylvania, wrote, "People don't buy term and invest the difference."[15] This strategy is a recipe for a guaranteed pay cut in retirement and a sig-

---

15   David F. Babbel and Oliver D. Hahl, "Buy Term and Invest the Difference Revisited," *Journal of Financial Service Professionals* 69, no. 3 (May 2015): https://www.academia.edu/31450051/Buy_Term_and_Invest_the_Difference_Revisited.

nificant loss of wealth for your family and the charities to which you might contribute in the future!

Term insurance can be benign or malignant due to its substantial wealth-eroding nature. Financial charlatans do not delineate between the two types of term insurance, yet understanding this difference can be the difference for you between the retirement of your dreams or one that is shrouded in financial uncertainty.

What is the difference between term life insurance that is diagnosed as malignant versus one diagnosed as benign? Early in dentists' careers, when resources are scarce and they still want the security of life insurance coverage, term insurance is appropriate as a short-term solution. If term insurance is carried throughout a dentist's career as a long-term strategy, it becomes very costly to own, as we just demonstrated in our example.

Term insurance that is owned in this manner is malignant and deadly to the dentist's long-term financial well-being. In order for term insurance to remain in a benign state, it must be eliminated from a dentist's Financial Treatment Plan as soon as possible. Often-times this is accomplished by converting the term insurance to a whole life policy. A key provision of a term policy is its conversion option. If term is purchased, it is important that you confirm that the policy has a conversion option to a whole life policy that allows the insured to convert from a term to a whole life policy in the future regardless of their health at the time. Eliminating the benign tumor, or term insurance, sooner than later prevents the term insurance from becoming malignant. Permanent insurance is all about living, while term insurance is only about dying. The last time we checked, dying is not a desired benefit for anyone.

As you age, and get closer to your mortality date, term insurance becomes much more expensive. Term insurance is often written in level term periods ranging from ten to thirty years. You will pay the least amount for a ten-year contract, while a thirty-year contract is the most expensive. For all the reasons illustrated in our example, a thirty-year policy is the most harmful.

If you are fortunate enough to live to the end of your level term period, your initial premium will then skyrocket, if you wish to keep the coverage. When you realize that your premium will rise substantially, you will drop the coverage. At that time, the premiums paid over the years, as well as the death benefit, are lost forever. It is like taking a million dollars off of your balance sheet and flushing it down the toilet. There is no way, unless you happen to die early, to benefit from term life insurance.

A death benefit that is guaranteed to remain in force until the day you die, is a turbocharger to your Financial Treatment Plan and a huge difference maker to your retirement. Owning permanent life insurance strategically positioned in your Financial Treatment Plan (discussed later in the book) will essentially allow you to spend your death benefit while you are alive. This will provide you with greater guaranteed income in retirement and allow you to pass your death benefit on when you die! Term insurance can have a place in your life as a short-term solution, but the long-term solution is permanent coverage.

THE MYTH OF COMPOUND INTEREST

A sacred principle in the traditional world of personal finance is compound interest. We have heard it called the million-dollar secret and it is commonly referred to as the eighth wonder of the world. The eighth wonder comparison has been attributed to Einstein (although there is no verification of this). However, being a nuclear physicist, it is likely that he was speaking of compounding numbers, and not interest or money. We think that economists, and even Einstein, would say that there is a big difference between math and money. Robert Castiglione coined the brilliant phrase, "Math is not money and money is not math."

One of the biggest drawbacks to compounding interest in any investment is the fact that when you compound interest back into an account, you only receive one use of that dollar. When interest earned simply goes back into an account, it is not seizing the opportunity to create a new asset or taking advantage of additional benefits within the Financial Treatment Plan. Compounding interest in a taxable account creates another problem: taxes must be paid on the interest, dividends, or capital gains earned by the account. These additional taxes are a real cost to the investment and must be considered when evaluating an investment decision. Let's examine a compound interest scenario and its overall impact on a dentist's financial well-being.

In this scenario, the dentist has invested $100,000 in an after-tax investment that is yielding 5 percent. The investment time frame covers a thirty-year time period and the dentist's tax bracket is 30 percent. Also, on the recommendation of the dentist's financial planner, the dentist will reinvest the annual interest earned on the investment in the account (see Figure 4.2 on the next page for a visual of this scenario).

TRADITIONAL COMPOUNDING

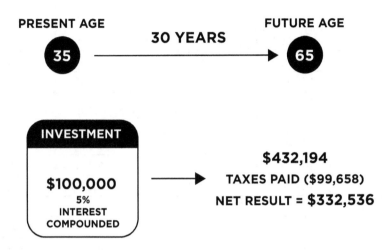

PRESENT AGE

35

30 YEARS

FUTURE AGE

65

INVESTMENT

$100,000
5%
INTEREST
COMPOUNDED

$432,194
TAXES PAID ($99,658)
NET RESULT = $332,536

ASSUMPTIONS
MARGINAL TAX BRACKET: 30%

Figure 4.2

At the end of thirty years the investment account will have grown to $432,194 due to the reinvestment or *compounding* of interest back into the account. In the traditional world of finance, this is where the analysis of compound interest stops. If the dentist likes the end projection of $432,194, he will move forward with this investment decision. Unfortunately, however, the dentist just made a financial decision without a complete set of facts. As with every other financial decision, when outputs are created, costs are generated as well, and the decision to compound interest is no different. As such, during the investment period, the dentist will also have paid taxes totaling $99,658 from another pocket for a net result of $332,536. This is the real economic result of compounding interest in this client scenario (see Table 4.3, on the next page).

YEAR	BALANCE B.O.Y. ($)	BALANCE E.O.Y. ($)	INTEREST EARNED ($)	ANNUAL TAX ($)	CUMU-LATIVE TAXES ($)
1	100,000	105,000	5000	1,500	1,500
2	105,000	110,250	5,250	1,575	3,075
3	110,250	115,763	5,513	1,654	4,729
4	115,763	121,551	5,788	1,736	6,465
5	121,551	127,628	6,078	1,823	8,288
6	127,628	134,010	6,381	1,914	10,203
7	134,010	140,710	6,700	2,010	12,213
8	140,710	147,746	7,036	2,111	14,324
9	147,746	155,133	7,387	2,216	16,540
10	155,133	162,889	7,757	2,327	18,867
11	162,889	171,034	8,144	2,443	21,310
12	171,034	179,586	8,522	2,566	23,876
13	179,586	188,565	8,979	2,694	26,569
14	188,565	197,993	9,428	2,828	29,398
15	197,993	207,893	9,900	2,970	32,368
16	207,893	218,287	10,395	3,118	35,486
17	218,287	229,202	10,914	3,274	38,761
18	229,202	240,662	11,460	3,438	42,199
19	240,662	252,695	12,033	3,610	45,809
20	252,695	265,330	12,635	3,790	49,599
21	265,330	278,596	13,266	3,980	53,579
22	278,596	292,526	13,930	4,179	57,758
23	292,526	307,152	14,626	4,388	62,146
24	307,152	322,510	15,358	4,607	66,753
25	322,510	338,635	16,125	4,838	71,591
26	338,635	355,567	16,932	5,080	76,670
27	355,567	373,346	17,778	5,334	82,004
28	373,346	392,013	18,667	5,600	87,604
29	392,013	411,615	19,601	5,880	93,484
30	411,615	432,194	20,581	6,174	99,658

Table 4.3

Tim

Many times, dentists are under the impression that if they want to improve their financial situation, they must first be willing to move their current investments to the newest and best products or investments available today. Now don't get me wrong, this can be the best situation in a limited number of cases due to high costs, unfavorable tax treatment, limited access, and minimum benefits, to name a few. However, in client situations we encounter, it is rarely necessary for a client to liquidate investments to reinvest elsewhere. As we stated earlier in our book, the products we own do not drive financial success. Instead, financial success is driven by the strategies we implement as supported by our products. The best financial decisions are not about *what* to invest in, but, rather, about *how* we position our money in the Financial Treatment Plan.

A question that Mart and I always ask ourselves when preparing a Financial Treatment Plan for a new client is, How do we improve the dentist's financial situation without adding new money or increasing the underlying risk for the dentist? At the same time, we want to find a second use (at a minimum) for each available dollar, which allows us to create additional assets, improve the plan's overall results, and add more benefits. A question to ask yourself is, If this type of planning is possible, why wouldn't I want it?

With these new objectives in mind, let's look at an alternative solution for the compound interest situation we just examined. The original investment of $100,000 remains unchanged. However, the annual interest earned on this account will not be compounded back into the investment. Instead, starting in the second year of the investment, the interest will be pulled out of the account at end of each year and moved into a Roth IRA using a back-door strategy. After year two, the $5,000 interest earned on the after-tax investment will be moved into the Roth IRA where it will earn the same 5 percent interest going forward. At the end of year thirty, the after-tax investment will have its original principal of $100,000 and the Roth IRA will have grown to $332,194. The total gross output for this scenario is the same $432,194 (see Figure 4.3 for a visual overview of this scenario).

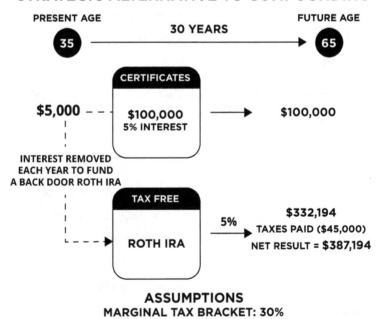

Figure 4.3

As with the original scenario we discussed, the alternative scenario also involved costs in the form of taxes paid in order to produce its gross output. In this case however, the total taxes paid were reduced to $45,000 because the annual taxable interest of $5,000 was removed each year from the taxable account and deposited into the tax-free environment of the Roth IRA. The annual tax in this scenario was flattened at $1,500 ($5,000 x .30) per year, over thirty years for a total of $45,000.

Using the same assets (but in a different way) produced a net result in this scenario of $387,194, versus a net result of $332,536 when interest was simply left to compound in a taxable account. The difference of $54,658 represents a 16 percent improvement as a result of finding an effective second use for the interest-earned dollars in the alternative solution. Can you imagine how the efficiency of your Financial Treatment Plan grows exponentially over time as you find additional uses for each dollar?

A final point to consider when examining these two scenarios is the potential income that can be generated from each result at retirement. Assuming a dentist retires at the end of the thirty-year period under review, how much income can these assets generate assuming an interest-only withdrawal at 5 percent? A detailed breakdown follows on the next page:

	INTEREST COMPOUNDED	ALTERNATIVE SOLUTION
After-tax investments	$432,194	$100,000
Roth IRA	- 0 -	$332,194
Total assets	$432,194	$432,194
INCOME GENERATED @ 5%		
Income from after-tax investments	$21,610	$5,000
Income from Roth IRA (taxable equivalent)*	- 0 -	$23,728
TOTAL INCOME	**$21,610**	**$28,728**

* The taxable equivalent assumes a 30 percent tax bracket.

Table 4.4

The point to take away from this example is that the alternative solution delivered the same gross output of $432,194, as compared to the compound interest scenario. The alternative solution, however, generated $332,194 of tax-free assets. This resulted in a $7,118 or a 33 percent increase in taxable income over the compound interest strategy. All of this was accomplished in the alternative solution without increasing the dentist's investment risk and with the reduced costs of $54,658 in the form of taxes paid. In addition, there were opportunity costs recovered on the tax savings. This is why financial success is not a simple math equation. If your planning is a simple math equation, you will lose the game and take a pay cut in your golden years.

For most, the debunking of these myths goes against everything they've ever been taught about money. But the four myths we've addressed, or debunked here, are just the tip of the iceberg. Making financial decisions based on these myths will cost you hundreds of thousands—and more likely millions—of dollars over a lifetime. Imagine recapturing this lost wealth at no out-of-pocket cost to you and your family! Hundreds of thousands—and possibly millions— more dollars to enjoy in retirement with less risk and the opportunity to be incredibly charitable.

The best way to test any financial decision is to measure it in an evidence-based way. When you have an economic model as the basis for a Financial Treatment Plan, results become very clear. With a Financial Treatment Plan you are able to measure and verify everything. It allows you to see the costs and the benefits of your financial decisions as well as the money gained and lost. More importantly, a Financial Treatment Plan allows an individual to cut through the sales hype and unfounded opinions that are rampant in the traditional financial world and make financial decisions solely based on economic facts. This is the only way to determine if a financial strategy is an economic truth or a myth.

Chapter 5

PUTTING YOUR
MONEY IN POSITION

• • •

*It's not how much money you make, but how
much money you keep, how hard it works for you,
and how many generations you keep it for.*

**—ROBERT KIYOSAKI, AUTHOR
OF *RICH DAD, POOR DAD***

Many dentists believe that a successful retirement is dependent solely on how big a retiree's pile of assets *is* upon retirement. Because of this view, most dentists we meet with have maxed out the retirement plans for both themselves and their spouse in order to accumulate those assets. Depending upon the cash flow of a dental practice, a dentist may even adopt a cash balance plan as part of an overall retirement plan. Also, as we've discussed, many dentists have been advised to accelerate their debt repayment, buy term insurance, and compound their interest. As proven in the last chapter, all of these recommendations are problematic for long-term wealth enjoyment.

If these pieces, which are part of many traditional financial plans, were the key to the retirement puzzle, dentists would be retiring earlier not later. The fact is that dentists today are retiring even later than before. A recent report on retirement published by the ADA found the average retirement age of dentists is now 68.8, up two years from just a few years earlier.[16] We find this statistic troubling for many reasons, but primarily because delaying retirement is sad and unnecessary.

The average dentist is now retiring close to age sixty-nine. That tells us that many dentists are needlessly missing out on the best decade of their life. A recent Stanford University study asked eighty-year-old couples, "If they could relive any decade over again, what would it be? " Their answer was overwhelmingly the decade of their sixties for four reasons: 1) their kids were out of the house, 2) they still had money, 3) their health was good, and most significantly, 4) they knew what was important in life!

Later retirement for the average dentist is happening despite the fact that dentists make a good income throughout their career and, typically, save a fair amount of money over their lifetime. This leads us to believe that the traditional way of positioning assets for retirement is seriously flawed.

The reasons that dentists delay retirement are numerous, but the most significant inhibitor to a dentist's long-term financial well-being is that it takes time for dentists to get their feet on the ground. Huge student loan obligations, starting or buying into a practice, purchasing a home, and perhaps starting a family can be significant financial obligations. This is on top of the fact that dentists are not able to start their earnings career until their mid to late twenties at the earliest. By default, the late career start will shorten the number of years available to accumulate wealth.

---

16 "2010 Survey on Retirement and Investment," American Dental Association.

A lack of understanding of the exponential curve of life is another factor that contributes to slow wealth creation and a later retirement date for many. By not knowing the importance of the exponential curve, and its impact on long-term wealth building, dentists set themselves up to lose millions of dollars before and during retirement.

EXPONENTIAL CURVE OF LIFE

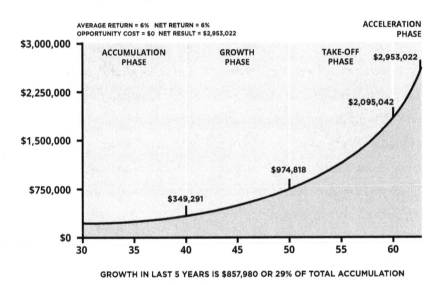

GROWTH IN LAST 5 YEARS IS $857,980 OR 29% OF TOTAL ACCUMULATION

Figure 5.1

Most dentists understand how the exponential curve impacts them in the accumulation phase of their life when they are investing in retirement plans or after-tax investments. The graph above depicts a thirty-five-year time period in which a person is saving $25,000 per year to a retirement plan at an assumed interest rate of 6 percent. New monies contributed to this plan will grow slowly during the accumulation phase or the first ten years of the curve. They pick up steam during the growth phase of the curve (between years eleven and twenty) and take off between the years twenty-one and thirty.

The most significant growth in this example, however ($857,980 or 29 percent of the total accumulation), occurs in the last five years of the curve during the acceleration phase. This graph clearly shows that. Every poor decision made early in a career impacts the end of the curve and, therefore, long-term wealth. The problem for most dentists, however, is that minimal to no consideration is given to the other wealth-building phases—distribution and conservation—and how the exponential curve impacts these. This is where millions of dollars are lost and why retirements are delayed.

It is our hope that you will no longer look at the three phases of wealth accumulation, wealth distribution, and wealth conservation as separate and distinct. You are now mindful that all three phases of wealth building are dynamically related and intertwined throughout your life. Every money decision that you make will impact at least two, if not all three, of these phases. Hopefully, we have impressed upon you the importance of this reality and why you want a Financial Treatment Plan to achieve maximum wealth.

The purpose of all long-term savings is to replace your income in retirement. Regardless of their age, it is imperative that all dentists know and understand the distribution strategy for their retirement accounts and other investments when they first decide to invest. In other words, distribution strategies should be discussed and implemented long before a dentist is ready to retire. In the traditional advisory world, as discussed in the last chapter, dentists are told to maximize their retirement plan contributions at the expense of everything else, with little understanding of how to get the money out thirty years later.

If no distribution strategy is in place at the time of retirement, which is true for most dentists we meet, then by default, a dentist is relegated to accepting an extremely low distribution rate for retirement income. What is a distribution rate? It is the amount of money that can be regularly withdrawn from retirement funds without risking the depletion of those funds during the retiree's lifetime. The simulations that measure these probabilities are called Monte Carlo.

On a side note, we find it funny that the financial industry uses the same verification method to determine the likelihood of not running out of money in retirement as casinos use to measure the probability of winning at the various gambling options they offer. The Monte Carlo simulation both reveals instances that have a high rate of success for the retiree to not run out of money and also shows the scenarios in which a casino will win big through gambling operations. Despite the statistics that are in favor of the casino, we all know people who have won while gambling. At the same time, we also know people who have run out of money in retirement. Our point is simply this: although a Monte Carlo simulation may show a high rate of success, it is not a guaranteed result and may fail. Knowing this, as a retiree, do you really want to base your retirement income on a Monte Carlo safe withdrawal rate? We think not!

As mentioned previously, in the traditional world of finance, where distribution rates are, typically, in the 2–4 percent range, dentists do not have enough time to accumulate the assets that will be required to replace their income in retirement. The solution to this dilemma is to position financial assets over the course of a career in such a way that the distribution rates are in the range of 7 percent (today's rate) to 13 percent (historical high) at retirement. This is a game changer. The retirement income will more than double and increased risk during the accumulation phase will not be incurred.

The proper positioning of assets in your Financial Treatment Plan takes significant pressure off the long-held belief that you need to accumulate a large sum of money in order to replace your income.

For example, dentists would only have to accumulate $3,750,000 in total assets at an 8 percent distribution rate to replace a $300,000 income. In contrast, a safe withdrawal strategy at 3 percent would require dentists to accumulate $10,000,000 by retirement in order to deliver the same income of $300,000. Achieving an increased distribution rate in retirement has very little to do with the investment's rate of return or even the financial product itself. Instead, it has everything to do with the strategy behind the financial products. Wouldn't it be great to not have to depend solely on the rate of return?

It is the marriage of your investments with actuarial science that provides the most income along with guarantees in retirement. What is actuarial science? It is a discipline that assesses financial risks in the finance and insurance fields using mathematical and statistical methods. It applies the mathematics of probability and statistics to define, analyze, and solve the financial implications of uncertain financial events. Life insurance, annuities, and pension plans are the main applications of actuarial science (see Investopedia, s.v. "Actuarial science," https://www.investopedia.com/terms/a/actuarial-science.asp).

The key to an actuarial-based (protected) asset strategy is that to ensure that the amount of the whole life insurance death benefit matches total invested assets at retirement. When this occurs, the only purpose of the retirement assets is to provide an income to the dentist at retirement (see flow diagram, below). This income can be fully maximized and guaranteed with a strategy that provides a 7 percent distribution rate for a sixty-five-year-old male today. The death benefit of life insurance addresses the longevity and estate issues of the wealth conservation phase and allows retirees to fully maximize and enjoy their retirement income today without the fear of running out of money.

Income is fully maximized in retirement when there is a 1:1 ratio of retirement assets to whole life death benefit. The presence of whole life insurance in the Financial Treatment Plan acts as the permission slip for dentists to take the maximum income from their retirement assets. If the money is positioned correctly over the course of time, there should be no additional out-of-pocket cost in order to double the income in retirement. In other words, lifestyle does not need to be changed to implement these strategies. The details of how one implements a protected asset strategy are discussed further in chapters 6 & 7.

Achieving these results is having a game board that provides an evidence-based way of determining where every dollar that comes into our lives should be positioned. The only way to do this is to have a Financial Treatment Plan. Let's take a look at how a Financial Treatment Plan is built from start to finish

A successful Financial Treatment Plan starts with having a solid foundation in place. If this foundation is ignored, or not complete, your financial house can and will crumble at the first occurrence of an unexpected event.

The three cornerstones that make up the foundation of a successful Financial Treatment Plan are maximum protection, a disciplined savings rate of 15 percent at minimum, and a cash liquidity position equal to at least 50 percent of one year's gross household income. We believe that if dentists achieved only these three objectives, they would be light-years ahead of the majority of their peers. Unfortunately, we have yet to meet any dentists who already have these three cornerstones in place when they become our clients. Obviously, a fully implemented Financial Treatment Plan is ideal, but if the foundation of the three cornerstones is missing, the treatment plan will fail at some point. Let's examine the three cornerstones.

The acquisition of maximum insurance coverage is the first cornerstone in the Financial Treatment Plan. Types of insurance coverage included in the treatment plan are: auto, homeowners, liability, disability, health, and life. Some may wonder what maximum insurance coverage represents. The answer is simple. Maximum insurance coverage is nothing more than owning the amount of insurance coverage you would want if the event you insured against were to occur.

As an example, if you were to injure someone in a car accident, how much liability coverage would you want to own? Also, if you became permanently disabled, how much disability income coverage would you want? If you were faced with a major health issue, would you want to own minimum or maximum health insurance coverage? Finally, in the event of your death, how much life insurance would you want to own in order to replace your income for your loved ones?

The amount of coverage desired is different for everyone, depending on the individual's situation. Most dentists would agree, however, that they would want to own the maximum amount of insurance coverage possible if they were to face any of these adverse situations. So shouldn't individuals own maximum insurance coverage today even though they don't know when such a situation is going to occur? The answer to this question is a resounding yes! Why is it, then, that most dentists don't already have the maximum possible insurance coverage? For most dentists, it all comes down to the perceived cost of acquiring insurance coverage. If cost were not an issue, however, would there be any reason not to own maximum protection at all times?

Ideally, these types of coverage can be acquired with little to no out-of-pocket expense to the dentist. Despite what the traditional world of finance will tell you, the cost savings in this area will result more from how these protection assets are purchased than the actual cost of the products themselves. Examination of the dentist's entire Financial Treatment Plan will allow for cost minimization strategies to be implemented in the acquisition of the protection assets.

A comment we hear often is, "I don't want to be overinsured." The fear of being overinsured is not realistic, however, as no insurance company would ever allow this to happen. An insurance company will only replace a specified loss of value and not a penny more. This is the purpose of the underwriting process for all insurance products.

The second cornerstone in the Financial Treatment Plan is establishing a disciplined savings rate of no less than 15 percent of one year's gross household income. If you have a gross income of $300,000, then we want to see $45,000 being saved in the Financial Treatment Plan. This is the target we strive for. The sooner you can get to that point, the better off you will be.

The 15 percent annual savings rate is a minimum target and is needed to offset the wealth-eroding factors of life that we all encounter and that include such things as inflation, taxes, planned obsolescence, technological change, and standard of living increases, to name a few. If a 15 percent savings rate is not obtained, then the dentist is actually going backward from an overall financial standpoint, due to these and other wealth-eroding factors. The discipline of saving is key to a Financial Treatment Plan's success.

The final cornerstone in the foundation of the Financial Treatment Plan and the third step to building a solid financial foundation is to establish strong liquid cash reserves. These reserves should be established even before starting to save funds in a retirement plan. Therefore, the initial goal with our savings is to establish a strong liquidity position. We like to see dentists maintain 50 percent of one year's gross household income in liquid funds. If you are making an annual salary of $300,000, then you want to have $150,000 in liquidity, or six months of your annual gross income. Liquidity can be held in checking, savings, CDs, or money market accounts, and it even includes the cash value of your whole life insurance.

Why do you need so much liquidity? The answer is that if you don't have liquidity, you don't have permission to do anything else in your Financial Treatment Plan. Liquidity is key! Liquidity covers unexpected emergencies and is available for possible investment and business opportunities.

• • • • • • • • • • • • • • • • • • • •

Tim

Years ago, a mentor of mine shared with me his belief that people all have one or two real opportunities fall in their lap at some point during their lifetime. Unfortunately, a high percentage of people never act on these opportunities. He concluded that the reason people don't take action is because they did not have the cash on hand to do so.

For those of you who may believe that maintaining a high cash reserve is inefficient, due to the low interest rate earned on savings today, you are missing the point. I believe that some of the highest rates of return are earned when a 0 percent rate of return meets opportunity. When you have cash on hand, you can react quickly. If you don't have cash on hand, you may miss the opportunity!

• • • • • • • • • • • • • • • • • • • •

The most important reason to maintain some liquidity, however, is to provide peace of mind. Life is a lot different when you have a strong liquidity position in place and the market goes down 30 percent. In this case, if you have cash on hand, you are not as panicked. You may even choose to make an additional investment when the market is down and stock prices are low. This is what successful investors attempt to do. On the other hand, if you only have $5,000 sitting in your bank account and the market goes down 30 percent, you are more likely to panic and make an emotionally charged decision to liquidate your investment account.

Keep in mind that if your liquidity is used for any reason, then it needs to be replenished to reestablish that peace of mind and give you the ability to respond quickly to emergencies and opportunities as they arise. Typically, it will take a dentist several years to establish a liquidity position equal to 50 percent of annual earnings, so do not think it has to be done overnight.

Once liquidity is established, the foundation of the Financial Treatment Plan is set. The foundation of maximum protection, disciplined savings, and solid liquidity protects a dentist against unexpected events and wealth-eroding factors that can destroy a Financial Treatment Plan if left unchecked. This gives dentists total peace of mind as they begin building their long-term future wealth.

In sports, it is often stated that "defense wins championships." We believe that the same holds true when building wealth successfully. The three cornerstones that make up the foundation of the Financial Treatment Plan are the defense of a successful treatment plan. Just as in sports, a Financial Treatment Plan with a highly productive offense will struggle and frequently lose if there are holes in the defense. In order for dentists to achieve maximum wealth, their Financial Treatment Plan needs both a solid defense and offense. Let's examine the rules that comprise a successful offense in a Financial Treatment Plan.

First, compounding interest in after-tax accounts should be avoided. The key takeaway here is that any time you simply put compound interest, dividends, or capital gains back into the same account, you are, in essence, forfeiting your right to use those dollars a second or third time in your Financial Treatment Plan. This results in reduced wealth and benefits. (Please refer back to chapter 4 where the money myth of compound interest was debunked.)

This is where the wealth freedom account (WFA) comes into play. The WFA is a separate checking or savings account whose sole purpose is to capture earnings from plan assets (e.g., interest, dividends, capital gains) or new monies that are being saved in the Financial Treatment Plan. To prevent these monies from being spent in your everyday life, this account is not comingled with your household checking or savings accounts. Instead, the WFA's purpose is to accumulate these excess dollars so that they may be moved elsewhere within the Financial Treatment Plan on a monthly, quarterly, semiannual, or annual basis. Money is moved out of this account to be used in new ways where additional rates of return and benefits are created. This generates exponential growth on your money.

It is at this point that retirement plans first come into existence as part of the Financial Treatment Plan. As stated earlier, it is not the first place your money should go. Nor should you direct 100 percent of your annual savings into a retirement plan. Instead, our rule for savings directed into retirement accounts states that an individual should contribute up to the level of the employer's match. In no case, however, should you contribute more than half of your annual savings rate. As an example, if you are saving at the minimum target rate of 15 percent, you should put no more than 7 percent into a retirement plan. This allows you to build a broadly diversified Financial Treatment Plan that includes retirement assets and other outside investments.

Another point to keep in mind is that all retirement accounts are considered part of the savings component in the Financial Treatment Plan. The savings component is where our safe money resides. As such, we should not take undue risks with these funds. They should be invested in a moderately conservative fashion to help ensure that the plan assets will be there when you are ready to retire. Retirement assets that experience a market correction can decimate plans for retirement.

Is the employer 401(k) match a good thing? Accountants love to tout the benefits of a retirement plan's employer match. Also, the media tells us all the time that an employer match is free money, but is it, really? Maybe yes, maybe no. If you are the owner of the practice and therefore the 401(k) sponsor, the employer match is not a big deal because you are the employer. What this means is that you are matching your own money, so it is not free money, as we are told. When you are an associate or work for a corporation, such as a dental service organization (DSO), the employer match on the plan is a bona fide match because the money is coming from the corporation, not you.

Once the retirement plan is established, any excess funds saved can be directed to the growth component or investment section of the Financial Treatment Plan. This is where your risk money goes, which includes financial assets such as bonds, stocks, and hard assets including collectibles, antiques, artwork, cryptocurrencies, real estate, and business ownership.

The ideal objective in the growth component is to diversify holdings that are invested in the core assets of this component. A heavy concentration in any one of the core assets, whether it is bonds, stocks, or hard assets, will place undue risk on your overall Financial Treatment Plan. Outside influences, such as declining interest rates, stock market corrections, a soft rental or real estate market, or unexpected challenges in your own dental practice, can absolutely devastate a Financial Treatment Plan if you are heavily concentrated in only one core asset of the growth component. You want to strive for balance and diversification among all these assets.

Again, any dividends, interest, capital gains, rental earnings from real estate, and excess income from businesses are captured and moved back through your WFA. As discussed earlier, when monies accumulate in your WFA, you will consider utilizing those funds in one of three ways: 1) to pay down debt, 2) to enhance your insurance coverage, or 3) to make additional investments elsewhere. Your decision will be thought out and intentional, rather than an automatic reinvestment of the dividend, interest, or capital gain that creates an increasing compounding tax over time (read chapter 4 on the compound interest myth). As money is moved elsewhere within your Financial Treatment Plan, the velocity, or money multiplier effect, will come into play as you get a second, third, and fourth use of your dollars over time. This is how the rainmakers make their money, so why shouldn't you do it that way as well?

Proper positioning and placement of each financial asset is essential for building wealth in the most efficient and effective manner. In addition, eliminating unnecessary costs and risks in your Financial Treatment Plan will add hundreds of thousands if not millions of dollars of additional wealth to your balance sheet over your lifetime. However, as stated several times previously in this book, the accumulation of numerous assets by retirement is meaningless if you don't have exit or distribution strategies in place that will turn those assets into an income stream. A seven-figure net worth means nothing if you don't have the ability to spend and enjoy those funds during your retirement without the fear of running out of money.

Your wealth potential is maximized when you fully embrace the underlying rules of the Financial Treatment Plan described in this book. If you choose to ignore any step in the process of the Financial Treatment Plan, or implement the steps out of order, you will not achieve the maximum results. More importantly, you will have limited use and enjoyment of your money over a lifetime.

Another key principle to embrace when building wealth is keeping your money in motion. In other words, every time you find an additional use for a dollar, you will pick up another rate of return and additional benefits that further enhance your wealth. Money that is moving through your Financial Treatment Plan is like blood in your body. When blood is not moving, it can clot and cause death. When money sits in one place for too long it gets stale and eventually rots due to the numerous wealth-eroding factors discussed previously. Stale or inactive money is the financial cancer that can decimate personal finances. The incorporation of a wealth freedom account within a Financial Treatment Plan is the key to curing this financial cancer. Monies flow continuously into this account and are then redirected to other parts of the Financial Treatment Plan, much as the heart pumps blood to different parts of the body.

Implementing these evidence-based rules takes a lot of pressure off your accumulated assets. Because the assets in the Financial Treatment Plan are balanced with actuarial science, you no longer have to chase an elusive rate of return in the hopes of building a huge pile of assets. The strategic, combined positioning of the assets in the Financial Treatment Plan is more important than the individual assets themselves. Ideally, these rules, along with keeping your money in motion, are essential to positioning your money for full income replacement with guarantees in retirement. This process also affords you the opportunity to retire sooner rather than later. The only way to do this is to have a Financial Treatment Plan to guide you down the financial path toward ultimate enjoyment of your money both today and in the future.

Chapter 6

LANDING YOUR MONEY SAFELY

• • •

Know what you own and why you own it.

—PETER LYNCH

According to an old adage, you should not spend your principal in retirement because you will need it to generate interest for the rest of your life. That adage simply does not hold water any more. It only works if you want to take a pay cut in retirement. Less income is obviously not the objective for anyone.

When we ask dentists how they expect to spend their money in retirement, most of them answer, "We are just going to live off the interest of what we have accumulated and we will be fine." In truth, they have not given any deep thought to what that statement actually means. According to a New York Life survey, 77 percent of respondents reported that they did not know how much they could withdraw annually in retirement without running the risk of outliving their assets.[17] The fact of the matter is that in the world we live in today, *nobody* can live off the interest generated by assets

---

17 "77% of Americans Don't Understand How to Safely Withdraw from Their Nest Eggs in Retirement," New York Life, April 26, 2016, https://www.newyorklife.com/newsroom/2016/withdraw-from-nest-eggs-in-retirement.

if income replacement is the goal. Whether it is saving accounts, laddered CDs, bonds, dividends, or any other investment, right now the interest earned by that principal would range from 1 percent to 4 percent. Honestly, will that interest allow you to have the retirement you want?

Let's assume you have accumulated $3,000,000 at retirement and use a 3 percent safe withdrawal rate for your retirement income. In this scenario, the investment will generate $90,000 of income each year. If you managed to accumulate that much money, in all likelihood, you were probably earning $250,000 to $300,000 a year as a dentist. If you planned on living off the income generated by interest in retirement, then the $90,000 of investment income in this example does not go very far in replacing your preretirement income. In fact, if you were looking to fully replace your income of $250,000 in retirement, you would have to accumulate roughly $8.3 million in assets. For many, accumulating this sum of money would be impossible due to either a lack of time or the inability to set aside this amount of savings.

The old adage of living off your interest in retirement may sound like a great idea, but in reality, this strategy will only set you up to lead a retired life of quiet economic desperation.

In the traditional financial world, where retirees' piles of assets are solely concentrated in their retirement plan, they will unknowingly have placed a lot of pressure on these assets to perform during the golden years and provide an income for as long as the retirees live. For a married couple, this income needs to provide for two lifetimes, which can each be as long as thirty-five years, or more in some situations. Running out of money is one of the greatest fears for a retiree.[18]

---

18 Ryan Derousseau, "4 Financial Fears About Retirement, And How to Overcome Them," *U.S. News & World Report*, January, 20, 2017, https://money.usnews.

No one should allow this to happen. If a retiree wants to leave a legacy to anyone, it will need to come from these assets. As a result, retirees are left trying to preserve capital for longevity or estate purposes at the expense of accepting an increased distribution rate for income during retirement. This situation is further complicated by the fact that a Monte Carlo distribution rate of 3 percent does not guarantee an income stream for life, as the assets will be spent over time. We believe this is unacceptable.

Upon retirement, many begin to realize that there is a lot of pressure on the pile of assets concentrated in their retirement plans. They also realize that they have no control over how this money will grow or diminish, because it is subject to market fluctuations, interest rates, and tax law changes. All of a sudden, they are living in a world of fear because they realize that they have minimal control over their assets. They remember the old adage and think, *Okay, we'll try to live off our interest.* Then, they quickly realize they can't do that either. Their next thought is, *I need to be in the market. My advisor tells me that the market has historically delivered over a 10 percent rate of return.* On average, this is true, but when was the last time you received the same rate of return year after year? Never! Market returns are variable. You may get a positive return one year and a negative return the next year, and so on. Remember 2008? This is a significant dilemma, as rates of return will fluctuate from year to year. During retirement, this volatility can have a dramatic impact on your golden years.

The accepted retirement option in traditional retirement planning is to take money at what is referred to as a safe withdrawal rate (Monte Carlo distribution), as discussed in the last chapter, from retirement assets. Years ago, these safe withdrawal rates were upward

---

com/investing/articles/2017-01-20/4-financial-fears-about-retirement-and-how-to-overcome-them.

of 7 percent. Even the legendary investor Peter Lynch said that a 7 percent withdrawal rate was an appropriate distribution rate for an all-stock portfolio.[19] Over time, a 7 percent withdrawal rate has proven to be way too high as markets go up and down unpredictably. Amazingly, 58 percent of people surveyed in 2016 still felt that a safe withdrawal rate in excess of 4 percent was acceptable, with 31 percent believing over 10 percent was safe.[20]

In today's world, the accepted safe withdrawal rate is between 3 and 4 percent. Without proper planning, dentists will fall into this trap at retirement. Unfortunately, due to volatile markets, low interest rates, and unexpected life changes, even at a low 3–4 percent withdrawal rate, there is still a chance that dentists and their spouse could run out of money if they live long enough.

Many of our dental clients are hoping to retire as early as age sixty. That means their money may have to last them for thirty-five years or longer in retirement, which could be longer than their entire working career. Consider this statistic: a 3 percent safe withdrawal over thirty years in retirement has successfully funded individuals and kept them from running out of money 97 percent of the time throughout the history of the market. If you live five years longer, for a total of thirty-five years, your chances of not running out of money during retirement now drops to 91 percent at that same 3 percent safe withdrawal rate. That means there is almost a one in ten chance that you will run out of money over a thirty-five-year time frame when using a 3 percent annual withdrawal rate. These numbers are obviously more ominous with a 4 percent annual distribution.

---

19   Peter Lynch, "From the Archives: Fear of Crashing," *Worth, March 9, 2017,* *https://www.worth.com/from-the-archives-fear-of-crashing.*

20   "77% of Americans Don't Understand How to Safely Withdraw from Their Nest Eggs in Retirement," New York Life.

Many of you may think that running out of money in retirement will never happen to you. After all, that's the kind of thing that happens to other people. Our question is—what if it *is* you? What do you do then? What is your back-up plan? What if you retire and the very next year there is a drop in the market, as there was in 2008, and you lose 40 percent of your investments? Does that change your retirement? The answer is a definite yes. Remember our wrapper discussion in chapter 2 and the objective to create plans that work under all circumstances. Failure cannot be an option!

● ● ● ● ● ● ● ● ● ● ● ● ● ● ● ● ● ● ●

Mart

I was at a conference where Steve Forbes was speaking. He said something along the lines of, "With all of the technological advancements in healthcare these days, the average lifespan will increase by ten to fifteen years."

Therefore, we may live much longer than we can even envision today. As a result, our greatest risk in retirement will be outliving our assets. We can't know how long we will live. This means that our retirement money may have to last a very long period of time. Therefore, having more guaranteed income, and not just a pile of assets, is key to a successful retirement.

● ● ● ● ● ● ● ● ● ● ● ● ● ● ● ● ● ● ●

Again, when we talk about the probabilities of running out of money, people always feel it will never happen to them. They believe they have smarter advisors on their team, or that they have the ability to see things coming. For a proper perspective on this, let's take finances off the table and consider another situation. Let's assume that you and your significant other arrive at the airport to leave for an extended weekend getaway. Before you board the plane, however, the pilot comes across the intercom and says, "I just checked the weather and we are going to have a fantastic flight, with the exception of a fifteen-minute period when we will be flying through some really dangerous storms. Don't worry though! I have done my calculations and there is a 90 percent chance that we will land safely on the other end." This means, of course, that there is a 10 percent chance that the plane will crash.

Knowing this, how many of you are willing to still get on that plane? Even with only a 10 percent chance of the plane crashing, when we ask a seminar audience this question, no one raises a hand to say yes. People would rather head to the rental car desk to rent a car or wait for the next flight.

Retirement can also be a life-and-death situation. If you wouldn't board a plane that has a 10 percent chance of crashing and ending your life, why would you take a 10 percent chance of running out of money during your retirement? Running out of money in retirement may not result in your death, but it most certainly leads to a living death.

It's interesting that people will accept the chance of running out of money in retirement, as if they have no other options. When getting on a plane, you want 100 percent certainty that the plane will land safely. Why wouldn't you want 100 percent certainty when it comes to your income in retirement as well? The reason may be that while the plane crash has a definite result (you know if that plane goes down, it is very unlikely you will survive), you may think that if you run out of money there will be a back-up plan.

You think, *Well, maybe the kids will step in, or maybe I can go back to work.* If you are running out of money toward the end of your retirement, however, it often means you are seventy-five or eighty years old. How employable will you be at that age? Will your skills still be up to par? How likely is it that you will be hired? Would you really want to ask your children to support you?

The biggest issue with a safe withdrawal rate of 3 percent, even if it were guaranteed to continue providing for the duration of your retirement, is the low income it yields in retirement. You are, essentially, saying, "Okay, I am going to make it, but I am not going to live life to its fullest." We think that is unacceptable. Why not have 100 percent income replacement *and* live life to the fullest? In the traditional financial world, you may make it 90 percent of the time, but you will be taking less income. Great, you made it, but you did not live the life you expected in retirement!

● ● ● ● ● ● ● ● ● ● ● ● ● ● ● ● ● ● ●

Tim

As an example, let's use a 3 percent withdrawal rate on $1,000,000 for the decade of the 1990s. At the end of those ten years, which hosted the greatest bull market in the history of the stock market, your million dollars would have grown to about $4,300,000 after withdrawing $30,000 annually for your retirement income. Life would have been great, and you probably would have been thinking that you could adjust and take more income annually.

The very next decade, however, from 2000 to the end of 2009—the so-called lost decade of the stock market—if you had withdrawn the same amount of $30,000 each year, you would only have had $593,000 in your retirement account balance at the end of ten years. This is an unbelievable but real difference, based on the sequence of market returns dilemma.

Now, let's look at the most recent decade, from 2008 to 2017. At the end of 2017, assuming the same annual withdrawal of $30,000, your account balance would total a little over $1.6 million. Most people would be happy with this result over a ten-year period. The problem is, at the end of 2008, or the first year of retirement in this example, the retiree's account balance would only have been $611,000 due to the stock market crash of 2008. Our bet is that people who were down almost 40 percent in their retirement account after the first year would not have stayed in this retirement strategy long enough to see the $1.6 million at the end of ten years. During the stock market crash, most retirees would have bailed out of their investments and done something different with their money. It then becomes an emergency, as you have less money and are staring at a reduced retirement income in the face. As a result, you are going to have to make some difficult decisions, such as downsizing your home, selling a second home, traveling less, dropping your country club membership, and making other cuts in your budget or lifestyle.

• • • • • • • • • • • • • • • • • • • •

Many dentists have very limited time to spend on financial planning. They are busy with their practice and life gets in the way.

Due to business, family, and other outside commitments, they have no time to meet with their team of advisors. Their practices are thriving, their children are growing up too fast, and all of a sudden, they are sixty years old and they have done very little to truly prepare for retirement. They find themselves in this position not because they have failed to take advice, but rather, the advice they did take came from the traditional retirement planning world where accepting a 50 percent pay cut in retirement is commonplace.

Up to this point, dentists have made and spent a lot of money and lived a great life but oftentimes were not diligent savers or saved money in the wrong places. Maybe they had a retirement plan, a practice to sell, possibly some real estate in the form of an office building, or a cash balance plan, in addition to other investments, but they have done no strategic positioning of their assets.

What's the answer to this? First, dentists have to understand that traditional retirement planning has significant problems. If they don't understand the problems created by their traditional retirement plans, they will never accept a solution for the problems. Our initial step is to help dentists better understand where they are financially today. We show them what they can expect if they continue on their current paths, based on the assets they have accrued at this moment. We also look at present contributions and any possible new money that dentists anticipate saving, going forward. Based on an assumed rate of return, and the number of years dentists have before retirement, they will now be able to visualize their current retirement path. We then allow them to discover that without an exit strategy in retirement, they will be looking at an income in retirement equivalent to a 3 percent withdrawal rate on their investments, and worse yet, accepting a retirement income that is not guaranteed. When this stark reality sinks in, dentists realize this is not the retirement path they want.

Once there is agreement that they do not want to stay on their current retirement path, the next step is to look at how they can solve their retirement dilemma using the same inputs and assets they have today. We are not talking about taking additional money from their pockets. We are instead helping them discover more efficient ways to use the same inputs in a Financial Treatment Plan that will create more long-term wealth and benefits with no additional out-of-pocket costs or increased risk.

These inputs can include money going into their savings accounts, retirement plans, or different investment accounts. Other inputs may include overpayments made on student loans or prepayments on their mortgage and other debts. We also look at the internal efficiency of assets already accumulated to date. For example, are interest, dividends, and capital gains being automatically reinvested in an after-tax account? It is our job to help individuals discover more efficient ways to use the assets and resources that are part of their financial lives.

In doing so, however, it is not appropriate for us, or anyone else for that matter, to simply say, "This is what you should do with your money" without first providing verification. You work hard for your money and financial decisions are too important to base them on opinion only. As such, you should demand verification from your advisors prior to making any financial decision. This is where our Financial Treatment Plan comes into play.

We start by analyzing the present money decisions made by a dentist. It is important to understand all of the positive results related to these decisions as well as any negative results that may exist. After all, if the net result of a financial decision were neutral or negative to your overall wealth building, wouldn't you want to know about that? Of course you would!

Once our dental clients are aware of their present situation, we introduce alternative strategies (using the same resources) and compare them side-by-side with the clients' present strategy. Using the Financial Treatment Plan, the positive and negatives results of each decision can be economically verified. As such, sales hype, opinion, and emotion are removed from the analysis. This allows dentists to make a financial decision based on economics and nothing else.

Through the use of the Financial Treatment Plan, our dental clients will discover the economic results generated from the placement of each dollar. Our goal is to create an exit strategy that will help our dental clients more than double their income in retirement. At the same time, we want to eliminate any possibility of our clients having to accept a safe withdrawal rate of only 3 percent at age sixty-five, with no guarantees. Instead, we want individuals to experience 7–8 percent (or higher) distribution rates from their assets at retirement, *with* guarantees.

How do we do that? Part of the answer lies in the incorporation of actuarial science as part of the Financial Treatment Plan. This was first mentioned in the last chapter and requires that whole life insurance and/or distribution specific annuities are part of the overall plan in some capacity. Ideally, we want to achieve a 1:1 ratio of the total whole life insurance death benefit to the total value of outside investments and retirement plans. If one area is more heavily weighted than the other, we will not achieve maximum results. In other words, it is bad to have excessive assets without life insurance, or to have too much life insurance without the assets. Balance is the key. These things are essential to fully replace preretirement income throughout retirement.

● ● ● ● ● ● ● ● ● ● ● ● ● ● ● ● ● ● ●

Tim

Too often what keeps dentists from adding whole life insurance to their financial plan is a perception that it's too expensive or that the advisor is going to receive a big commission to their detriment. As are the many myths we have discussed, these beliefs are misinformation promoted by traditional advisors, accountants, and financial gurus. As an example, in Plan A, a dentist is contributing $50,000 to his retirement plan and investments. In Plan B, a dentist is contributing $50,000 that is allocated between a retirement plan, investments, and whole life insurance. Is there any difference in the total annual savings entering plan A or Plan B? The answer is no. What is expensive is not having all three asset types in the Financial Treatment Plan at the time of retirement.

● ● ● ● ● ● ● ● ● ● ● ● ● ● ● ● ● ● ●

To achieve multiple streams of income in retirement, it is absolutely necessary that during their working years, dentists allocate their annual savings equally to their retirement plan, outside investments, and whole life insurance. Let's examine some of the possible income streams that are available after retirement.

The most obvious income stream that every dentist receives at retirement (assuming the program remains viable) is Social Security. We believe this to be true for dentists who are within ten years of retirement today. Unfortunately, for dentists starting their careers today, Social Security will likely be different by the time they retire.

Other income stream possibilities include interest or dividends from investments, income streams from annuities, spend-down strategies on assets, and maximum versus minimum distributions from a retirement plan. Rental income from an office building or other properties can also be a great income stream during retirement. Additionally, you could have a charitable trust that produces income (more on this later). There might also be collectibles, cryptocurrencies, and master limited partnerships. Almost anything that produces income can be an income source. In reality, you could have ten or more different sources or streams of income in retirement. When this happens, you are positioned to receive an income that resembles roaring rapids rather than a trickle.

Most working dentists that we encounter are on the path of only receiving a trickle of income in retirement. This is because they will have only three to four sources of retirement income. These typically include Social Security, a retirement plan, and proceeds from a dental practice sale. If dentists happened to own the building they practiced in, they may add a rental income in retirement. To fully replace the dentist's income, however, there should be many more streams of income!

One question we are often asked is, if you are taking the same dollars and allocating them in different places within the Financial Treatment Plan, how do you not end up with just the same money in the end?

If you had a choice of accumulating either $1,676,000 (Dentist A) or $1,267,000 (Dentist B) of assets at retirement, which dentist would you choose to be? The obvious choice here is Dentist A with $1,676,000 in assets. I mean, who would not want an additional $409,000 of assets in retirement? For most, having the biggest pile of assets at retirement is the goal they have been advised to chase.

Using the same set of facts, you are now informed that Dentist

A can only derive an income of $50,000 a year from accumulated assets after retirement. This is due to the fact that no exit or distribution strategy is built into Dentist A's plan and by default, she is forced to accept a 3 percent safe withdrawal from her assets in retirement. Not only does this method provide minimum income to the retiree, but the income is not guaranteed, meaning it is subject to market and interest rate fluctuations throughout the dentist's retirement years. As a result, Dentist A is not able to fully enjoy her retirement assets.

On the other hand, Dentist B did build a retirement distribution strategy into his Financial Treatment Plan using actuarial science, so at retirement he could receive $67,000 a year in income from his total assets of $1,267,000. In addition, the annual income for Dentist B is 100 percent guaranteed. Knowing this additional information, which dentist would you choose to be now, Dentist A or Dentist B?

Without exception, with this new information, individuals will unanimously choose to be Dentist B in retirement, as they want more income to spend and enjoy. Having more assets in retirement means nothing if it does not equate to more retirement income. There are only two types of income in retirement; one that is guaranteed and one that is not guaranteed. Most retirees prefer guaranteed income if given a choice. Guarantees provide peace of mind and eliminate the uncertainty and related stress induced by market corrections and interest rate fluctuations that can and will occur during a dentist's retirement years.

Some may ask, how is the scenario described above even possible? After all, Dentist B has $409,000 less in assets at retirement, but more income to spend and enjoy. As we said earlier in this book, you should always demand verification of financial alternatives. With that in mind, let's verify each of these financial alternatives for Dentist A and Dentist B.

In our example, both dentists are thirty-five years old, and we are examining a thirty-year time frame until they reach age sixty-five. The dentists' assumed tax bracket is 30 percent and their investment rate of return is 6 percent. In this scenario, each dentist is saving the equivalent of $20,000, pretax, each year. They have identical situations but choose different financial paths.

Dentist A is simply saving her $20,000 each year into her retirement plan. Over a thirty-year period at a 6 percent rate of return, Dentist A's retirement account will grow to $1,676,000 by age sixty-five. Again, this is a large sum of money, but keep in mind that this money is essentially inaccessible until retirement.

Dentist B, on the other hand, takes those same dollars but only directs $11,500 to his retirement plan each year. At age sixty-five, assuming the same 6 percent rate of return, Dentist B has accumulated $964,000 in his retirement plan. The remaining $8,500 of pretax money, or in this case $5,950 of after-tax money (assuming a 30 percent tax bracket) was directed to the purchase of a whole life policy on Dentist B that has an initial death benefit of $472,000. At age sixty-five, the whole life death benefit on Dentist B will have grown to $668,000 and its cash value will be $304,000. Thus, at age sixty-five, Dentist B will have amassed total cash assets of $1,267,000 and have a whole life death benefit of $668,000.

At sixty-five, Dentist A will have a retirement plan with $1,676,000 and nothing else. Dentist A has no exit or distribution strategy built into her plan and by default she will accept some form of a safe withdrawal rate (Monte Carlo distribution) from her retirement plan assets. Today, that accepted withdrawal rate is 3 percent, or in this example, $50,000 of retirement income each year.

• • • • • • • • • • • • • • • • • • •

Tim

When retirement assets by themselves are the sole income source, a lot of pressure is placed on them due to three factors:

1. The retirement assets have to provide an income stream throughout the retirement years. Desire for income in retirement does not go away because the market happens to experience a 20 percent market correction. It can be devastating to a retiree when the market takes a hit like this and the retiree still needs income to survive.

2. The retirement assets need to last a lifetime. In other words, retirees will be in trouble if the assets are exhausted before their death. If they are married, then these assets must support two lifetimes and not just one. Depending on their age at the start of their retirement, they could be dependent on these assets as long as thirty-five years, or longer. Remember—retirement can last longer than a career.

3. A legacy (e.g., left to a spouse, children, or charities) must also come from these assets, which may cause the retiree to preserve principal at the expense of taking an adequate income in retirement.

If not addressed properly and eliminated in retirement, these three factors will add undue stress. As we have said, due to one or more of these retirement pressures, most retirees are leading quiet lives of economic desperation, which will be your retirement world, too, if the bulk of your retirement income is derived at a safe withdrawal rate.

● ● ● ● ● ● ● ● ● ● ● ● ● ● ● ● ● ● ●

Dentist B, however, is in a much different situation at retirement. This is due to the fact that he owns a guaranteed whole life death benefit of $668,000 (tax-free) at age sixty-five. This tax-free death benefit will pass on to a spouse, children, or charities at the time of his death. In essence, the tax-free death benefit takes care of any legacy considerations that Dentist B may have. As a result, all the retirement plan assets have to do is provide an income stream to the dentist and his spouse that will last over their respective lifetimes.

In this example, this was achieved on a guaranteed basis by trading the retirement plan assets of $964,000 at age sixty-five for a single premium immediate annuity (SPIA) with a single life option on the dentist only. In today's interest rate environment, this will provide an annual guaranteed income stream of $67,000 ($964,000 x .07). This income is paid as long as the dentist is alive. Upon the death of the dentist, the life insurance death benefit will be paid out to the named beneficiaries (e.g., spouse, children, or charities) to replace the assets that were spent in retirement. The strategy described here is what we refer to as a protected asset strategy.

Now, when we look at the two retirement income options for Dentist A of $50,000 per year and Dentist B of $67,000 per year, which one would you want? Both results for Dentist A and Dentist B were achieved with the same annual inputs, yet Dentist B realized a $17,000, or 34 percent, increase in income at retirement. Also, Dentist B's income is 100 percent guaranteed and not subject to market risk. The icing on the cake for Dentist B is that the dividends on his whole life policy can be used as another income stream if necessary. Unfortunately, Dentist A cannot say the same for her retirement income. Most dentists clearly want to be Dentist B, who has more retirement income—income that is guaranteed—and enjoys the certainty that any legacy concerns have been addressed.

Please keep in mind that the solution shared in this example is one of many possible alternatives and is dependent upon individuals' personal situations as well as their wants and desires. In other words, there is no one-size-fits-all solution when it comes to retirement planning. The key is having flexibility and more options to choose from.

A big fallacy in the investment world is that in order to achieve a high rate of return, you have to take more risk. This may be true in the microeconomic world, but not in the macroeconomic world. Why not have more money and more income with less risk? (That is one of our wealth objectives discussed in chapter 2.) The above example proves that premise very clearly because it considers the big picture. In other words, you can have more income in retirement without chasing a high rate of return and assuming more risk when efficient distribution strategies are built in to the Financial Treatment Plan.

One last thing: when assets are macroeconomically positioned in a Financial Treatment Plan, the total assets accumulated will be virtually the same as those accumulated under a traditional plan. This means that, as Dentist B, you can have your cake and eat it, too, by having the $1,676,000 of assets that Dentist A has, *plus* a $1,676,000 (taxable equivalent) death benefit. This would then position you to have a possible retirement income of $117,000 per year ($1,676,000 x .07) that is 100 percent guaranteed without considering the cash values or dividends related to the whole life policy! The sweet spot from a positioning standpoint is having a 1:1 ratio of your assets to your permanent death benefit. This is how you prevent a pay cut in your golden years!

Returning to the plane analogy where the objective is to land safely at your destination, if you want to land safely with your money in retirement, then your financial decisions need to be integrated and coordinated to achieve maximum benefits and outputs today and in the future. Just like the pilot who performs a preflight check before takeoff and then closely monitors in-flight progress to ensure a safe flight, this same attention to detail should be given to your personal finances.

Chapter 7

IS YOUR RETIREMENT INCOME A SURE THING?

• • •

When it comes to retirement income, there are only two kinds of income: guaranteed or not guaranteed. It is really that simple. Yet, these income options are rarely discussed. If they are, it is usually at the end of a dentist's career when the options for securing maximum income are more limited. Dentists must figure out what portion of their retirement income they want guaranteed. Some dentists want a guarantee on 100 percent of their income. Others say, "I really do not need that much guaranteed, but I would like a portion guaranteed to cover my monthly expenses." In the end, it is a personal decision. However, many of the dentists we work with like the idea of a guaranteed basic income.

Mart

If dentists can go into retirement knowing that their basic monthly expenses are fully covered by guaranteed income sources, then they can have tremendous peace of mind regardless of fluctuations in the stock market or interest rates. It also gives them permission to still invest in the market if they choose to do so with their remaining assets.

Why would a client not want guaranteed income? It comes down to the presence of the rainmakers and the tremendous misinformation that is presented to dental professionals. Types of guaranteed retirement income are, basically, limited to Social Security, pensions, and annuities. If the system is not changed by 2034, a 21 percent reduction in benefits will be necessary to sustain the program.[21] Knowing this, Social Security may not be as guaranteed in the future as it has been for so many up to this point. Also, pensions, such as cash balance plans, are not a viable option for guaranteed income in the dental world, as very few dentists actually have one. That leaves annuities as a form of guaranteed income in retirement.

Annuities can be complicated and confusing. There are many investment advisors, financial planners, and accountants who say you should not have an annuity under any circumstances. Ken Fisher, one of the biggest money managers in the country, markets with a passion against annuities, using the word *hate* in regard to them. This is nothing more than marketing. There is absolutely nothing to hate about a guarantee. As we have said throughout this book, there is no magic financial product. When you look behind the curtain of advisors who are telling you that they hate a product, you can be certain you will find they have an agenda to sell you something else.

In the simplest sense, an annuity is a financial contract issued by an insurance company that provides a series of guaranteed payments to the owner. These payments can be received for a specified period of time or over the lifetime of one or more individuals. Annuities do exactly what corporate pensions do for eligible employees. Purchasing an annuity can be likened to creating a self-made pension:

21   Jeanne Sahadi, "Social Security must reduce benefits in 2034 if reforms aren't made," CNN, June 5, 2018, https://www.cnn.com/2018/06/05/politics/social-security-benefit-cuts/index.html.

An individual trades some assets for a stream of guaranteed income. An annuity is a great tool for those looking for secure sources of income in retirement. Unfortunately, when other advisors discourage annuities, this only creates confusion. The response from the client becomes, "Oh, I don't want that."

For most dentists, it is not that they do not want guaranteed income in retirement (because practically everyone *does)*. A TIAA-CREF study reported in 2016 that 73 percent of those surveyed wanted to secure their retirement nest egg.[22] We feel that many people choose not to put money into an annuity because they do not understand it. Many are led to believe that money placed into an annuity is forever lost at death. With proper strategies in place, however, this does not have to be the case.

One of the reasons that annuities have received such a bad name is that they have been used improperly for many years. They have been pitched as an accumulation tool by financial institutions and that is not what they were designed for. Annuities were designed as a distribution tool. This is a big difference! Any time you try and use something in a manner other than what it was designed for, it is going to be inefficient. It would be like using a slow-speed handpiece to cut a preparation for a filling knowing that a high-speed handpiece is a more efficient way to get the job done. You wouldn't do it. Buying an annuity for accumulation is the same thing. There are much better ways to accumulate money than purchasing an annuity.

This brings us to one of the main themes of this book: How are your financial assets positioned? As we discussed in chapter 5, the positioning of your assets is key to determining how much income

---

22 "TIAA 2016 Lifetime Income Survey: Executive Summary," TIAA-CREF, September 14, 2016, https://www.tiaa.org/public/pdf/C33638_Lifetime_Income_ExecSummary.pdf.

you will receive in retirement. Making an investment without understanding where the financial asset should be positioned in your overall Financial Treatment Plan will cost you a lot of money today and income in the future. All Americans, including dentists, want the gold standard of achieving a full income replacement at retirement. That is our objective for our clients.

As discussed in the last chapter, the largest retirement income stream is achieved by using a protected asset strategy. This strategy requires that permanent whole life insurance be part of the Financial Treatment Plan. Ideally, you would want to have a 1:1 ratio of your total assets to your whole life death benefit (taxable equivalent) at retirement.

For example, if you have $2,000,000 between your retirement plan and outside investments, then the whole life insurance death benefit on a tax-equivalent basis should equal $2,000,000. In today's interest rate environment, a protected asset strategy in this situation would generate approximately $140,000 at a 7 percent pay-out rate of annual guaranteed income over a lifetime. Upon death, the taxable equivalent death benefit of $2,000,000 or more is paid out to the named beneficiaries (e.g., spouse, children, charities) to fully replace the assets that were spent down in retirement.

The protected asset strategy is possible when the dentist owns whole life insurance and purchases a SPIA with a single life option using retirement funds or other invested assets at retirement. The drawback to a SPIA with a single life option, however, is that this income stops the day you die. Upon your death, any money left in the annuity goes to the insurance company. Although this option will provide the highest income while you are alive, if you do not live very long, the insurance company wins big at this game. Also, if legacy is a priority for you and your spouse, then whole life insurance must be a part of your Financial Treatment Plan in order to elect this income option at retirement.

Although a protected asset strategy provides the highest level of guaranteed income for a retiree, not everyone will pursue this option for various reasons. Nonetheless, if dentists still like the idea of having some guaranteed income in retirement, then they can consider either a SPIA with a joint life rider or a basic annuity with an income rider. Each of these options will provide a reduced level of guaranteed income based on the same $2,000,000 of assets used in the example above. Depending on the dentists' personal situation, one of these options may be the right fit. One thing is certain, if whole life insurance is not part of a dentist's Financial Treatment Plan, the dentist will take a pay cut in retirement. Please refer to table 7.1 that summarizes the various income options in retirement based on having $2,000,000 of assets.

INCOME PRODUCT / STRATEGY	DISTRIBUTION RATE	INCOME GUARAN- TEED?	INCOME PROVIDED FROM $2M OF ASSETS	LEGACY PROVIDED FOR
Protected asset strategy	7%	Yes	$140,000	Yes
SIPA, joint life	5.75%	Yes	$115,000	No
Annuity with income rider	4.5%	Yes	$90,000	Maybe
"Safe" with- drawal or Monte Carlo distribution	3%	No	$60,000	Maybe

Table 7.1

The next retirement option to provide guaranteed income at retirement is a joint SPIA. The income provided by a joint SPIA is payable over two lifetimes (typically, the lifetimes of a husband and wife) and will be less than the income paid under an SPIA with a single life option. If a husband and wife are both sixty-five years of age, the distribution rate today is 5.75 percent. Using the same $2,000,000 of retirement assets, a joint SPIA would provide $115,000 of guaranteed income today. This income will stop at the death of the second covered person. If there is any money left in the annuity, the remaining amount will revert back to the insurance company.

Dentists are enticed when they initially look at these first two guaranteed income options because either one will give them the highest income when looking at multiple choices. But upon further analysis, they realize that if they were to die early in retirement, these options could possibly disinherit their loved ones and the charities to which they hope to contribute. Legacy is provided for a spouse with a joint SPIA option. However, if the dentist and spouse also want to provide for children or charities, then when an SPIA option is elected, whole life insurance should also be adopted as a protected asset strategy in the Financial Treatment Plan. If legacy for children or charities is not a concern, then permanent life insurance is not required.

The final guaranteed income option that we will discuss is an annuity with an income rider. This annuity option is similar to the first two options discussed in that it can produce a guaranteed income over one or two lifetimes. However, it is unique in that if you die with assets still left in the annuity, the remainder goes to your named beneficiaries and not the insurance company. Due to this unique benefit, the income rider on the annuity will offer a reduced distribution rate on the assets placed in the annuity. Today, that guaranteed distribution rate is approximately 4.5 percent for a sixty-five-year-old. Using our previous example of having $2,000,000 of assets at retirement, this will result in $90,000 of guaranteed income each year. In summary, this annuity option will provide guaranteed income for a dentist in retirement without the dentist losing control of assets in the annuity, but at a reduced distribution rate. As we always say, every financial product has advantages and disadvantages.

• • • • • • • • • • • • • • • • • • •

Tim

The income options we just discussed use annuity products to provide effective distribution or income strategies with guarantees at retirement. This is the primary strength of an annuity product and why we refer to them as wealth distribution tools. Unfortunately, just as a lot of things in the world of traditional finance do, products oftentimes end up being promoted as the end-all solution for all financial issues. As we said earlier in this book, there is no such thing as a magical financial product that solves all financial issues.

Despite this, the financial world often promotes the use of an annuity as a wealth accumulation tool by hyping the perceived benefits of a variable or fixed equity-indexed annuity. Benefits often pitched are tax deferral for after-tax assets invested, protection against market losses, suit protection, and a death benefit, to name a few. The question to always ask when making a financial decision is, At what cost am I getting these benefits?

Possible disadvantages to consider when purchasing an annuity for wealth accumulation *only* are the loss of capital gains tax treatment for after-tax assets invested, back-end load surrender charges of up to ten years, and a 10 percent early withdrawal penalty from the IRS on taxable funds withdrawn prior to age fifty-nine and a half. Other disadvantages include limited investment options and, in the case of an indexed annuity, potential earnings lost in a rising market due to low caps or high interest rate spreads. This is why some pundits say they hate annuities.

To reiterate, if accumulation is your sole objective, there are more effective products than variable and equity-indexed annuities. If, however, you are interested "in the rest of the story," as Paul Harvey used to say in his daily radio commentaries, there is no better product than a correctly used annuity when it comes to wealth distribution or guaranteed income replacement.

● ● ● ● ● ● ● ● ● ● ● ● ● ● ● ● ● ● ●

Most dentists who desire a guaranteed income source in retirement will select one or a combination of the three annuity distribution options discussed. In addition, depending on their legacy concerns, they may also incorporate a protected asset strategy into their Financial Treatment Plan. If they choose not to go down one of these paths, then, by default, they will accept a retirement income that has no guarantees to support it. This means adopting a controlled, spend-down strategy—spending down principal and interest over a specified period of time—or taking a Monte Carlo safe-withdrawal distribution. Neither option provides a guarantee of success and both can be easily sidetracked in a down market.

In a controlled, spend-down strategy, dentists make assumptions about 1) the rate of return they expect to earn on their retirement assets, and 2) the length of time they want those assets to last. Again, let's assume that a dentist has $2,000,000 in retirement assets at age sixty-five, which he will invest in a conservative portfolio at 3.5 percent. His time horizon for this money would be twenty-five years, or age ninety. Based on the assumptions given above, he would then withdraw principal and interest of approximately $117,000 each year from retirement assets until it was spent down to zero at age ninety. Now, many of you may already recognize the glaring problem with this strategy: if it works as planned and the dentist lives beyond age ninety, he may be out of money. Worse yet, he could run out of money before age ninety if he happens to retire in a down market. Either way, if the dentist outlives his money, not only has he lost his income but there will also be no legacy for his spouse, children, or charities.

In summary, a controlled, spend-down strategy is never one that you would use with 100 percent of your retirement assets. With that being said, it could be effective for a portion of your retirement asset balance in combination with other retirement income strategies.

The last retirement income option we will discuss is the widely accepted and promoted Monte Carlo safe-withdrawal distribution from retirement assets. In this strategy, dentists leave their retirement assets fully invested and hope to maintain, or even grow, their retirement asset base while pulling out a safe withdrawal to live on in retirement. This withdrawal, which may be inflation adjusted, is made each year regardless of whether or not the retirement portfolio had an investment gain or loss. The idea behind this strategy is that in the long haul, dentists can take out income each year without depleting their retirement assets and still leave a legacy to loved ones or charities when they die.

From a historical perspective, a safe withdrawal strategy works most of the time, as confirmed by any number of Monte Carlo simulation calculators available on the internet. A great internet calculator that supports this statement is Vanguard's Retirement Nest Egg Calculator. The one big issue with this strategy, however, is that in order to have a 98 percent likelihood of not running out of money in thirty years, the safe withdrawal rate for dentists can be no more than 3 percent of their retirement assets. Using our previous example of having $2,000,000 of assets at retirement, this would result in a retirement income of only $60,000 annually, none of which would be guaranteed. Even if a 3 percent safe withdrawal strategy could ensure that dentists would not run out of money in retirement 100 percent of the time, it would be unacceptable, due to the low income allowed. Therefore, a safe withdrawal strategy is very inefficient for a retiree.

● ● ● ● ● ● ● ● ● ● ● ● ● ● ● ● ● ●

Tim

Throughout our many years in private practice, Mart and I have seen, many times, other advisors recommending a safe withdrawal rate of 4 percent and even higher. Historically, as verified by Vanguard's internet Retirement Nest Egg Calculator, this withdrawal rate of 4 percent is successful only 91 percent of the time over a thirty-year period, based on a portfolio consisting of 50 percent stocks and 50 percent bonds. From another perspective, this means that dentists and their spouses would have a one out of ten chance of running out of money during a thirty-year retirement period. Going back to our earlier airplane analogy, if you knew that you had a 10 percent chance of not landing safely at your destination, would you get on that plane? If the answer is no, then why would you take this same chance in retirement?

● ● ● ● ● ● ● ● ● ● ● ● ● ● ● ● ● ● ●

Many traditional advisors who do not like annuities often recommend some form of a safe withdrawal strategy to provide dentists an income in retirement. They may also recommend other investment strategies to provide the same retirement income. They present their plans by saying, "You can structure your stocks to live off dividend income," or "You can ladder your CDs," or "You can live off your bond interest," to name a few. That is how they sculpt their plans for their clients, but none of these investment strategies are guaranteed. These plans for retirement income are based on a hope and a prayer. If inflation and interest rates are running high, then these eroding factors can devastate a fixed income portfolio. This is the most common option that we see offered by traditional planners, and it provides the least income with greater risk and no guarantees. In baseball, that is a strikeout!

The other thing that comes into play is that the compensation of most advisors in the traditional financial world is based on assets under their management. For some, giving up control of those assets by placing them into an annuity may mean they will give up future compensation from those assets. The business of a stockbroker or investment advisor is focused on maintaining control over a client's assets and managing them, on a fee basis, for twenty to twenty-five years. This underlying objective can prevent advisors from supporting an annuity, a financial strategy that would give their clients increased income and real guarantees in their retirement. Since so few stock brokers and advisors are fiduciaries—who are required by law to do what is in the best interest of their clients—there is little incentive for the stock broker or advisor to expand their clients' knowledge base, which may include recommending an annuity. This is one reason why the government has become involved, from a regulatory perspective, to promote the fiduciary standard.

● ● ● ● ● ● ● ● ● ● ● ● ● ● ● ● ● ● ●

Mart

As a sidebar, only 10 percent of financial advisors in America are fiduciaries, which is shocking. The other 90 percent of advisors are not held to the same standards. Another name for an investment fiduciary is a registered investment advisor (RIA). We, as doctors, have a fiduciary standard to do what is right for the patient, so why don't we have the same expectations of our advisors? In his book *Unshakeable,* Tony Robbins warns that if your advisor is not an RIA, "Smile sweetly and say goodbye." Tony asks, "Why would you ever choose a financial advisor who doesn't have to act in your best interests over one who does? You wouldn't!" Yet many dentists still work with advisors who are not fiduciaries. We agree with Tony that it is very important to work only with fiduciaries when making financial decisions.

● ● ● ● ● ● ● ● ● ● ● ● ● ● ● ● ● ● ●

Oftentimes, a major reason dentists do not choose a SPIA with either a single or joint lifetime income option is that they are afraid they will disinherit their loved ones. All legacy concerns are addressed, however, with the ownership of whole life insurance as part of an individual's Financial Treatment Plan. The inclusion of whole life insurance gives you permission to take a higher income in retirement. You can spend and enjoy the assets you worked so hard for all your life and enjoy life to its fullest in retirement. You will have guarantees and peace of mind, knowing that when you die, your life insurance is positioned to fully replace the assets you have spent, whether for your spouse, your kids, or your favorite charity. In baseball, that is a home run!

Successful Financial Treatment Plans are built on strategy, not on products. Even if we found our clients the ideal investment product that delivered a 10 percent rate of return every year, and our clients put all of their money into that investment, they would still lose. Why? Because it is very inefficient to build an exit strategy with only one product. It is almost like a one-person band versus an orchestra. An orchestra with many musicians is going to create more beautiful music than one person playing an instrument alone. In the financial world, when you have a balanced and diversified Financial Treatment Plan, you will have many more options and flexibility to deal with what you face today and in the future. Again, it is not about getting the biggest rate of return. Many times, a moderate rate of return with more benefits is a better option than the home-run investment with a higher rate of return and more risk.

● ●

Tim

Another important issue to understand is that having a strategy alone is not enough. The financial institutions, media, and advisors all promote many different financial strategies that they claim will ensure financial success. Oftentimes, upon full analysis in the Financial Treatment Plan, these same strategies make no economic sense. There are a number of strategies that are totally inefficient from a wealth-building standpoint. They include the strategy to buy term insurance and invest the difference and the strategy to continually compound interest. Both are very inefficient strategies that we see many dentists employing in their financial lives, thinking they are doing the right thing. Instead, they are going in the wrong direction or simply treading water. It is not about *what* product you own but, rather, *how* that product is used in your Financial Treatment Plan that, ultimately, determines financial success.

● ●

In conclusion, we want to circle back to the importance of not taking a pay cut in retirement. Also, do you want a retirement income that is guarantee based through actuarial science or probability based through investments and Monte Carlo simulations? How much of a sure thing do you want? If you wait until you are sixty or older to answer these questions, you will have a more difficult time creating a viable retirement income picture because your options will be more limited due to a lack of time. Possible income guarantees also get watered down when dentists are late to the game in planning for their retirement. When planning for retirement, don't delay! Get started now. *It is what makes your golden years golden!*

Chapter 8

MAKING YOUR GOLDEN YEARS GOLDEN

• • •

Don't let making a living prevent you from making a life.

—JOHN WOODEN

While dentists are hardworking individuals, the fact that they are busy should not get in the way of their creating a life of significance. Throughout this book we have emphasized the importance of having a holistic Financial Treatment Plan. We have also shared some major strategies for income replacement in retirement, but the most powerful strategy involves giving money away to charity. Most dentists are aware of the concept of giving or tithing and the significant impact it can have on our communities, our faith, and society as a whole. Traditional financial planning, however, rarely includes charity in the planning process. Surprisingly, with the proper strategy, giving to charity can mean that you will have more money than if you do not give. That bears repeating, if you do not give, you will have less! It sounds counterintuitive, but as we have said previously, it is not the financial product, but the strategy behind the product that makes you successful. Including charity in your personal plan is a must and here's why.

Dentists want to be charitable, but they are hesitant. Many fear that if they are charitable, they may not have enough money for themselves or they may reduce their family's inheritance. While charity is important to most dentists, they hold reservations about giving.

The reason charitable giving is one of the most powerful distribution strategies is because it is the ultimate triple win. We call it this because if dentists choose to be charitable, they can position themselves to 1) have more income in retirement, 2) avoid disinheriting a spouse or children, and 3) make a gift to the charity of their choice while they live. In this way, everybody wins and nobody loses, a triple win.

Now many of you are probably thinking, how is it possible to increase wealth by giving it away? After all, this is counterintuitive to what we know and understand. In the traditional world, we know that when a check is written to charity, a tax deduction is received. However, the donor's overall wealth is also reduced by the amount of the gift. This is a basic and limited charitable strategy that involves one move of money and creates one benefit: a tax deduction. A triple-win charitable strategy is only achieved once the second, third, and sometimes a fourth move of the money are coordinated with the initial gift. When this occurs, additional benefits of tax savings, increased income, additional wealth, and the preservation of a legacy are possible.

Let's analyze a simple strategy we call turbotithe and compare it to traditional giving. Charities, including churches, schools, and other organizations are always looking for donations. These donations are most commonly made in the form of a cash payment via a check. A direct cash donation to a charity is a very inefficient way to give, even though it may be the easiest. With this in mind, let's compare a direct cash donation (Dentist A) to giving away an appreciated asset under a turbotithe strategy (Dentist B).

It is not unusual for a dentist to own a stock, bond, or mutual fund that has appreciated. When this investment is eventually sold, a capital gains tax of up to 23.8 percent (federal only) will be due upon sale. Wouldn't it be great if the capital gains tax on the sale of this investment could be eliminated? Absolutely!

For this example, let's assume that both dentists have $10,000 in cash and own $10,000 in ABC stock with a cost basis of $5,000. Both dentists believe that the ABC stock is a good one and want to continue owning the stock going forward.

DENTIST A

Dentist A simply writes a $10,000 check to his charity of choice and retains ownership of the ABC stock that currently has an embedded $5,000 capital gain. If Dentist A elects to sell his ABC stock in the future, and assuming the present market value of the stock remains unchanged, Dentist A will then recognize the $5,000 capital gain and pay a $1,190 capital gains tax ($5,000 x .238).

The result: Dentist A gave $10,000 to charity and pays $1,190 of capital gains taxes upon the sale of the ABC stock.

DENTIST B

Dentist B, on the other hand, donates the ABC stock, worth $10,000, to the charity. This means there is *no* tax on the gain from appreciated assets. At the same time, Dentist B takes her cash of $10,000 to purchase $10,000 of ABC stock or some other investment if she wants to rebalance her investment portfolio. The bottom line is that

Dentist B still owns ABC stock (or a different investment), but it now has a new cost basis of $10,000.

The result: Dentist B gave $10,000 to charity and reestablished the cost basis of the ABC stock (or new investment) at $10,000. By handling the donation in this manner, Dentist B eliminated the current capital gains tax of $1,190 on the original ABC stock and still owns the stock.

To summarize, the turbotithe strategy eliminates the capital gains tax on the appreciated asset *and* increases the cost basis of the retained investment holding by repurchasing the stock or new investment. It's a win-win strategy for the charity and the dentist. Without exception, *everyone* who writes a check to charity should consider this strategy. It is not always possible to do so, however, without a having a well-balanced plan.

The turbotithe strategy is excellent for smaller donations. When larger donations are considered for charity, more sophisticated and powerful strategies are available. These strategies often include advanced charitable planning tools, such as a charitable remainder annuity trust (CRAT) or a charitable remainder unitrust (CRUT). Do *not* attempt to implement these strategies on your own. At the very least, your accountant/CPA, and other outside planning experts (e.g., attorneys, professional personnel from charitable foundations) should be involved. You must comply with all IRS regulations if you want a good result with a charitable planning strategy.

• • • • • • • • • • • • • • • • • • •

Mart

Considering an advanced charitable planning strategy requires going back to what Tim and I have preached throughout this entire book: you must have a properly balanced Financial Treatment Plan. If the bulk of your assets at retirement are held only in a retirement plan, you will be severely limited in your charitable planning options. The type of advanced strategies we're discussing here are much more effective, and you will have more options if you have diversification in your asset holdings. In other words, besides a retirement plan, you will want to own other after-tax outside investments such as stocks, bonds, mutual funds, and real estate. Charitable planning strategies are enhanced even more if these outside investments have appreciated and have long-term gains built into their market value. The long-term capital gains tax on these assets can be completely eliminated with a charitable planning strategy while increasing your retirement income at the same time. This is why financial success comes from diversifying all your assets and not just owning stocks and bonds held inside a retirement plan.

• • • • • • • • • • • • • • • • • • •

In working with our dental clients, we want to know how they are wired. What are their passions in life? What is close to their heart, whether it be their church, synagogue, alma mater, or other charitable institutions that they may have worked with over the years. If they have a charitable intent, we plant a seed early in the planning process, letting the client know that there could be some very effective charitable strategies in their future. The beauty of these strategies is that you can experience a triple win by having more income in retirement, leaving a larger legacy to loved ones, and contributing to a charity of your choice all because you chose to be charitable while alive.

Regarding the last point, some recognition definitely goes along with making a donation to charity while you are alive. Many people place charitable organizations in their estate plan so that the charity benefits from their donation when they die, but that means they never get to see the results of their gift.

If you had your choice, wouldn't you rather make a gift to charity while you are still alive? Your gift may actually be the one that spurs others to do the exact same thing. The bottom line is that you feel great about helping a charity that is near and dear to your heart, and you get to witness the results.

When a triple-win charitable planning strategy is fully analyzed, it becomes apparent that those who choose not to give will actually be worse off than if they did.

Let's use some real numbers and examine a situation in which a charitable trust is used as part of a dentist's overall retirement planning. As we go through this example, it is important to note that the assets mentioned in this example do not represent the dentist's entire asset base at retirement. In other words, the dentist will have more assets that are held in some type of retirement plan (e.g., IRA, 401(k)) as well as additional after-tax assets.

In this example, we are looking at Dentist A and his spouse, who are both age sixty-five. The combined federal, state, and local tax rates for income and capital gains are 40 percent and 20 percent, respectively. In addition, Dentist A has $150,000 in a retirement plan and $1,000,000 of after-tax assets at retirement (see Figure 8.1). In the traditional world of finance, Dentist A would be looking at an annual income of $34,500, based on a 3 percent safe withdrawal strategy. This is a situation we see all the time.

TRADITIONAL INCOME PLAN AT 65

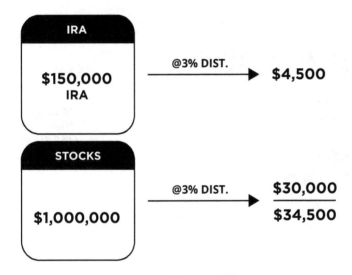

Figure 8.1

Now using the same facts from above, let's examine a charitable planning strategy for Dentist A and his spouse. This scenario allows the couple to make a sizable charitable contribution and increase their retirement income at the same time (see Figure 8.2). This strategy will require several moves in order to maximize its effect.

CHARITABLE GIVING STRATEGY

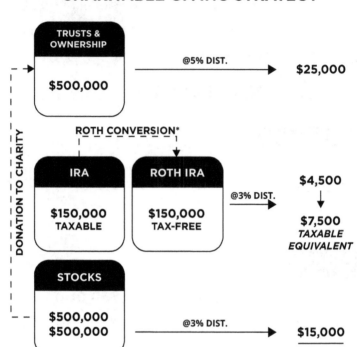

* THE TAXES OF $60,000 DUE ON THE ROTH CONVERSION ARE FULLY
OFFSET BY THE TAX BENEFIT CREATED THROUGH THE CHARITABLE DONATION.

Figure 8.2

The first move in this strategy requires Dentist A to gift $500,000 of his after-tax assets to a charitable remainder annuity trust (CRAT) that benefits his charity or charities of choice. Dentist A and his spouse are now the income beneficiaries of the trust. In this situation, Dentist A established the trust to provide a fixed 5 percent distribution (based on the original gift amount) or $25,000 each year. Upon the death of the second spouse, any remainder in the trust will pass on to the charity.

Due to the charitable contribution, Dentist A will receive a charitable tax deduction for that year of approximately $150,000. Because the $500,000 gift is a future gift and not an immediate gift to the charity, Dentist A will receive a discounted tax deduction based on the anticipated future value of the ultimate charitable gift. Based on the facts of this example, the tax deduction will approximate 30 percent of the original gift amount or $150,000. In a 40 percent income tax bracket, this will result in a tax savings to Dentist A of $60,000 for that year. For many, this is the point where their charitable strategy ends. In our example, however, Dentist A is going to take this charitable strategy to the next level by achieving even more benefits.

Dentist A enjoys a second use, or move, by using the tax savings created from the charitable contribution to offset the additional income taxes generated when he converts his IRA to a Roth IRA. In a 40 percent income tax bracket, the $150,000 Roth conversion will generate an additional $60,000 of income taxes. Since the charitable gift was made in the year that the Roth conversion was completed, Dentist A has, essentially, completed the Roth conversion with zero tax consequences. Dentist A now has his retirement money in a Roth IRA, which will provide tax-free income distributions going forward. Assuming a 3 percent safe withdrawal distribution, the Roth will provide him an additional $4,500 of tax-free income during retirement. In a 40 percent income tax bracket, this is equivalent to $7,500 ($4,500/.60) of taxable income.

The last piece of this strategy is the annual income provided to Dentist A from the remaining $500,000 of after-tax assets. Again, assuming a 3 percent safe withdrawal distribution, these assets will provide another $15,000 of annual income to Dentist A.

The total taxable equivalent income provided to Dentist A and his spouse under this ultimate charitable planning strategy is $47,500 ($25,000 + $7,500 + $15,000). This represents an additional $13,000 ($47,500 - $34,500) of annual income for Dentist A, who chooses to be charitable.

In summary, if Dentist A elects to use an ultimate charitable planning strategy based on the facts in this example, he will achieve a double win by increasing his retirement income by $13,000, or 38 percent, plus he will provide a gift to a charity. The third leg of the triple win, which is maintaining or increasing his legacy for his loved ones, should already be in place if Dentist A owns whole life insurance as part of his existing Financial Treatment Plan. If this is not the case, and legacy is important to Dentist A and his spouse, then an additional move can be incorporated into the charitable strategy to acquire whole life insurance.

So why don't all dentists do this? One reason is they don't know about it; no one has ever talked to them about how to accomplish a charitable gift with a win-win-win strategy. Charitable donations have always been thought of as a transaction wherein individuals make a gift to charity for which they receive a charitable tax deduction, but nothing else. This is microeconomic thinking!

Another reason that charitable strategies are rarely used in planning is that the idea or concept was not introduced early enough in the dentist's career. Ideally, you want to have these strategies on the radar, if not already positioned, anywhere from five to fifteen years before retirement. This time frame allows dentists time to position their assets in their Financial Treatment Plans in order to take full advantage of this planning strategy. It still works when you are older. However, it may be a bit more challenging, and you may only get a double win versus a triple win when being charitable.

• • • • • • • • • • • • • • • • • • •

Mart

The use of a charitable strategy in combination with a traditional retirement plan (401(k), or IRA) can allow dentists to receive a tax deduction upfront on their contribution, a tax deferral on all growth inside the plan, and, finally, tax-free access to their investments at the end. Dentists can only receive all three of these tax benefits through the strategic positioning of assets within the Financial Treatment Plan. Without strategic planning, they will, at most, only receive two of the three tax benefits as highlighted in the following table.

	TRADI-TIONAL 401(K)	ROTH 401(K)	OUR CHARI-TABLE PLAN
Tax-deductible on contribution	YES	NO	YES
Tax-deferred on accumulation	YES	YES	YES
Tax-free on distribution	NO	YES	YES

Table 8.1

• • • • • • • • • • • • • • • • • • •

It all comes down to building options. The better you are positioned, the more options you will have in the future. Good positioning gives you the freedom to make proactive decisions with your money. It also allows you to be the person you want to be, by giving you the opportunity to be charitable. Finally, giving while you are still alive is much more rewarding than having the donation distributed upon your death. In the end, contributing to a charity is the most powerful distribution strategy, so consider giving more.

Note: The example presented in the above charitable planning strategy is for discussion and informational purposes only. Do not rely on this for accuracy, as you must first consult your own attorney and other professional advisors to determine what may be best for your individual needs.

Conclusion

THE FINANCIAL ENJOYMENT FACTOR

• • •

"The journey to financial freedom starts the MINUTE you decide you were destined for prosperity, not scarcity—for abundance, not lack. Isn't there always been a part of you that has known that? Can you see yourself living a bounteous life—a life of 'more than enough'? It only takes a MINUTE to decide. Decide now."

—MARK VICTOR HANSEN, BEST-SELLING AUTHOR

This book started with a fight for your money, but it is ending with the enjoyment of your money! Its purpose is to introduce information that offers you the opportunity to avoid taking a pay cut in retirement, and at the same time build guarantees into your retirement income. This is the Holy Grail of retirement income planning, but it cannot be attained in the traditional financial planning model. This information is so atypical to what people are spoon-fed by the financial institutions and media that you must have an open mind to accept it. After all, having more income in retirement with guarantees offers you the opportunity to enjoy your retirement on many levels. It also means you get to do what you want without any reservations!

In order to achieve the above objectives, you will need to change your traditional, microeconomic mind-set—one that is often taken in retirement planning—to a more holistic, macroeconomic view. The strategies presented in this book embody a significant paradigm shift from the traditional way of doing things. The traditional world of financial planning is primarily focused on accumulating assets with minimal to no consideration given to the distribution phase. Also, let's not forget about the rainmakers: the government, financial institutions, and corporations. Each of these institutions is in an ongoing battle with individuals for control over their money. Hopefully it is clear to you now how important it is to never relinquish control of your assets.

Planning for the end of your dental career is much more than just accumulating assets. Sure you want to have a big pile of assets, but you want to do it in the most efficient way possible. This means that, throughout your career, you want to build in distribution or exit strategies that will allow you to fully enjoy—both today as well as in the future—what you have worked so hard for.

Our goal is for you to have full income replacement when you stop working rather than taking a pay cut in retirement, as most dentists do. Why take a pay cut when you don't have to? Why not position yourself to fully enjoy life in your retirement and still have enough money to leave the legacy you desire to your loved ones?

Dentists seemingly accept a 50 percent reduction in income upon retirement because that is what everyone else is doing. It's like watching lemmings going over a cliff one by one. Taking a pay cut in retirement is unacceptable. In order to avoid this, you will have to embrace the fact that you cannot accumulate enough assets over your working career to fully replace your income in retirement.

The rainmakers' success comes from understanding the velocity of money and not from accumulating assets. We want you to become the rainmaker of your own success. Instead of succumbing to the rainmakers' recommendations, you need to start thinking as they do. Learning how to multiply your money using the velocity of money principle will change your financial life. You need to be open-minded so that you are ready to take action. Changing your path from a traditional financial path to a holistic, evidence-based Financial Treatment Plan may feel foreign to you at first, but it is the path that will lead to 100 percent income replacement in retirement.

In order to change your financial path, the first step is to change the way you think about money. Think about what you *want* in life, not what you *need*. Unfortunately, traditional advisors focus on needs and goals, as does Suze Orman, "the personal financial guru," who proudly states that she is "the queen of needs versus wants." Needs are weak. In reality, all we really need are food, water, oxygen, and shelter. Goals are also somewhat weak because they are limited to the established goal. Wants and desires are powerful and limitless! Dentists do not come up short in retirement because they don't make enough money during their careers. They take a pay cut in retirement because they have fallen prey to the weak and inefficient strategies promoted by financial institutions, the media, and financial entertainers.

The second step to changing your financial path is to recognize who the rainmakers are and start acting as they do instead of being their victim. There are published books and even a commercial that talk about quantifying a number, the amount of money you may need at retirement. That is an exercise in futility! If you are forty years old today, how do you determine that number when your retirement is twenty to twenty-five years down the road? You don't know what inflation will be over that time. Will your family situation be different in the future from what it is today? What will your experience be in the stock market? Will interest rates change dramatically? How about tax rates? Do you think they may be different from what they are today? Yet, you are being asked to identify a number for a future retirement that may be twenty-five years away. Why not just make the decision that you are going to plan for a maximum income in retirement, and whatever that maximum amount is, that is the best you can do. We guarantee that a maximum amount will be a whole lot better than your perceived need, number, or goal is today.

We call this reaching your maximum financial potential. Just as athletes strive to reach their maximum athletic potential, we want you to meet your maximum financial potential. Unfortunately, you can never do that if you live in a needs-based world. It is impossible! Instead, focus on your wants and build your Financial Treatment Plan with those desires as the foundation. What do you want? Identify your wants and desires first if you want to live a happy and successful life.

Step three to changing your financial path is to know that you need a macroadvisor. You will not be able to reach your true, maximum financial potential without having a skilled advisor to lead and direct a team of advisors who will engage you throughout your lifetime. There may be dentists who accumulate a lot of assets, but they do so at the expense of having no exit strategy in place. As a result, they will get minimum enjoyment from their money in retirement. They will also be exposed to all kinds of risks, which may cause their money to disappear overnight because they don't have guarantees built into their financial plans. The do-it-yourselfers will never achieve their maximum financial potential.

As a dentist, if you have a cavity, are you going to stand in front of a mirror, drill that cavity out, and fill it yourself? Not a chance. You will go to a colleague and have that professional do the dental work. In the same vein, why wouldn't you want professionals on your team, helping you become financially successful? The answer for most is that an advisor burned them in the past, or they witnessed their parents' self-made financial success. For some, their ego gets in the way of accepting advice.

Do-it-yourselfers are the most limited when it comes to financial planning because they do not engage any advisors. As a result, they unknowingly place themselves behind the eight ball. They are penny wise and pound foolish because they think they are saving on fees and commissions. In the end, however, they are going to be very disappointed with their results. Trying to be a Lone Ranger with your personal finances will sabotage your financial future. We all need a Tonto by our side!

Then there are dentists who engage a traditional advisor who is only focused on helping clients accumulate wealth or build the biggest pile of assets. Again, we also want to accumulate maximum wealth, but if it is done at the expense of building effective wealth distribution and conservation strategies in the Financial Treatment Plan, you will lose. Traditional advisors live in the world of accumulation and linear thinking. Their focus is on accumulating assets in a retirement plan. Also, they usually only recommend term insurance to cover their clients' life insurance needs. As we discussed earlier in this book, if you enter retirement without owning at least some whole life insurance in your Financial Treatment Plan, you will take a pay cut in retirement.

The traditional path of financial planning is very inefficient and is directly responsible for the plight of most dentists today, who are retiring on roughly 50 percent of their preretirement income. These are your fifty-percenters! Remember the 50 percent analogy at the beginning of this book? It is a failing grade. Unfortunately, it is far too common to see dentists, today, who are in their fifties and wondering why they are not further ahead financially. Worse yet, they know in their gut that they are headed for a huge pay cut in retirement.

Change is difficult, and changing the way you think about your money can make you extremely uncomfortable. Money is a very emotional topic, and when the decision comes down to emotional or financial reality solutions, emotions will, unfortunately, win in most people's lives most times. A general rule to consider is that we all tend to gravitate toward the path of least resistance. In the world of personal finance, this means that decisions are often made based on what everyone else is doing. If this is an effective way to make financial decisions, then why are so many dentists struggling financially today?

Too often, dentists just stay with their plan to avoid the discomfort of change, but this decision comes with a significant loss of wealth and life-enjoyment today and in the future. Hopefully, we have presented in this book the reasons that will spur you to consider, and ultimately commit to, making that change!

• • • • • • • • • • • • • • • • • • •

Mart

Years ago, before I met Tim, I attended a financial seminar during my residency in Michigan. The person leading the seminar had a certificate that I had to sign at the end of the meeting. It was my promise that I was going to make a change in my financial life.

For whatever reason, signing that certificate made me feel good. Prior to this meeting, I had never really been exposed to or taught about personal finances. I can remember thinking, as I signed that certificate, that I was going to commit to learning more about how money worked and how I could best make money work for me and my family. That was the start of my lifelong journey of learning about financial information. The signing of that certificate taught me one of the most important things in life, which is commitment. I invite you now to make that same commitment to learning more about your personal finances and how you, too, can reach your maximum financial potential.

● ● ● ● ● ● ● ● ● ● ● ● ● ● ● ● ● ● ● ●

We have no problem saying that you should not have read this book if you cannot make a change. Unless you are committed to take action, reading the advice in this book is, quite frankly, a waste of your time. Talk and information are cheap without action and implementation. To produce the results we have discussed in this book, the commitment from you must be there, but that change may be uncomfortable at times. Hopefully we have provided you with a deeper understanding of the implications of not changing. Most people cannot afford the consequences of inaction.

If you are thirty-five years old, you may think that you have plenty of time to get your personal finances in order before you retire. The fact is those years are going to pass more quickly than you can imagine. Before you know it, you will be staring retirement in the face.

Instead of letting time pass, why not use it to your advantage? In order to best use the time, you must change how you think. You cannot take action on these principles and strategies until you open your mind.

A first step to opening your mind is to ask each of your advisors to verify and support every recommendation they make when it comes to your finances. As we have explained throughout this book, every financial decision will have an output, benefits, and, most importantly, costs associated with it. You should expect a full account of all three of these factors before committing to any financial decision. Also, is each financial decision in your Financial Treatment Plan coordinated and integrated with all others? In other words, is there a synergy between your financial decisions that is moving you forward financially, or are they stalled or even moving you backward? If you do nothing else, you should at least learn to expect a full account of the output, benefits, and costs of your financial decisions. As Ronald Reagan once said, "Trust, but verify, watch closely, and don't be afraid of what you see!"

The ultimate objective of this book is to open your mind to the very real possibility that you can fully replace your income in retirement with guarantees and still have the opportunity to donate to charity without reservation—in other words, to live life on your terms. This is the enjoyment factor.

If this is of interest to you, and you want to learn more about how to change your mind-set to achieve the perfect smile in retirement with a Financial Treatment Plan that demands pay-cut prevention for your golden years, please contact us at our website: yourretirementsmile.com, or call us at 1-800-281-0703. We are also happy to answer your questions at info@macro-wealth.com.

Finally, for those of you who are curious about your retirement readiness, please take our assessment at **www.yourretirementsmile. com** to see how close *you* are to retiring without taking a pay cut in your golden years.

Acknowledgments

There are a number of people we would like to acknowledge for their part in making this book possible. It is safe to say, however, that if it were not for Robert Castiglione and his passion for finding, explaining, and verifying the truth when it comes to financial decision making, we would not be putting these words to print. He invented and developed the system we use today. The power of this process is that it has stood the test of time over many decades and many different economic environments without having to change to accommodate the whims of the market or the economy. We are not aware of any other financial system that can do this.

Bob's ability to challenge the status quo and not accept the misinformation that is so prevalent in the financial planning world has helped thousands, and likely millions, of people across America reach their maximum financial potential. We are blessed to know Bob as a friend and to have his wisdom cross our paths years ago.

If it were not for Bob and his system, Tim would have washed out of the financial services world, as have so many other advisors searching for the truth. In March 1994, when Tim first saw this financial process for creating wealth, he knew within fifteen minutes that he had finally found what he was so desperately seeking for his clients. If Tim had not discovered this process, Mart would not have experienced this system and learned how it could benefit his family and the dental community.

We would like to recognize all our clients, who, after experiencing this process, say, "Why haven't I heard this before," or "It sounds like a no-brainer to me!" or "This makes so much sense." Dentists who are open minded and motivated to make a change embrace this system very quickly and appreciate the verification process behind it. Also, those dentists who engage in this process are significantly financially ahead of their peers and colleagues who continue to do what is recommended in traditional financial circles.

In addition, we would like to thank our mentors and friends who have further helped in shaping who we are and what we do. Without a strong network of mentors for lifelong learning, which includes people such as Al Dickens, Mike Welker, Lucian Ioja, Gabor Nagy, Mike Steranka, Brian Gengler, Art Sanger, John Smallwood, Pat Sweeny, Dave Connelly, and many others, we would not be the advisors that we are today!

Finally, and most importantly, we would also like to thank our spouses, Julie and Lindsey, for their unconditional love and support as we travel across the country lecturing, attending meetings, or holding evening webinar meetings with clients. Their support and understanding has made it possible for us to help as many people as we have. As Warren Buffet once said, "The difference between a golden egg and a goose egg in retirement is the chick you marry!" There is a lot of truth to that statement!

In closing, successful people realize that they need to surround themselves with people who help to advance their lives, from spouses, to friends, to team members, mentors, and business colleagues. We are THANKFUL and GRATEFUL that these people have helped us in more ways than we can put into words. Please, from the bottom of our hearts, enjoy our book!

About Macro Wealth Management

Dr. Mart McClellan and Tim Streid are presidents of Macro Wealth Management. The firm's niche is the dental and medical professions. Both Mart and Tim are registered investment advisors and each brings a unique perspective to their practice. Mart is still practicing as an orthodontist, and Tim has a strong professional background as a CPA. Their knowledge and experience creates a lot of trust with the clients they serve all over the United States.

Mart and Tim utilize an economically based financial model to create short- and long-term financial strategies for dentists. The foundation of their success is the use of a macroeconomic strategy that is based on economic principles and not opinions. Macro Wealth Management is the only dental-focused financial firm in the country that uses this model. Mart and Tim have lectured nationally and internationally to large and small groups. They welcome future opportunities to speak with groups of any size.

TIM STREID

Tim entered the wealth management business in 1989. By the end of 1993, Tim was disillusioned and considering a new career path, like many individuals who pursue a career in financial services. Tim was disillusioned and considering a new career path. Tim had been trained, as an auditor, to look at a company's entire set of books before signing off on an opinion. Because of this, he was frustrated when he entered the traditional world of finance and found that it did not embrace this same approach when helping clients to make life-changing financial decisions.

Instead, Tim was asking clients to make financial decisions based mostly on sales hype and opinion (as promoted by the financial institutions) rather than informing them about a comprehensive process that allowed them to discover and verify the best financial decisions for their personal situations. Tim knew there had to be a better way. Fortunately, in March 1994, Tim was introduced to the planning system and process that he still uses to this day. This planning process changed his life, and more importantly, the financial lives of his many clients. Throughout his career, Tim has continued to develop and hone a business philosophy that approaches wealth management from a unique, holistic perspective.

Tim serves as president of Macro Wealth Management and is a registered investment advisor. He graduated from Eastern Illinois University in 1984 and began his career working as a CPA with the big-four public accounting firm of Peat Marwick. Tim has spoken on personal finance at numerous speaking events all over the United States.

Tim resides in Peoria, Illinois, with his wife, Julie. They have three children: Taylor, Mark, and Grant. They have been actively involved in their children's athletic activities over the years and have officially joined the ranks of empty nesters now that their youngest son, Grant, has entered college.

In addition to his passion for his family and helping others achieve financial success, Tim also lends his time to improving his community. He is active in several organizations as well as his church. Tim is also an avid golfer and enjoys the lake life with his family.

MART MCCLELLAN

Mart McClellan brings a unique perspective to the financial advisory profession because he is not only a financial advisor but also a practicing orthodontist. Mart received his dental degree from Northwestern University and completed his orthodontic residency at the University of Michigan. His undergraduate degree was procured at DePauw University, where he discovered dentistry while on mission trips to Kenya and Guatemala.

After having a number of financial advisors, he was referred to Tim by a fellow dental school classmate. Tim introduced Mart to the unique, holistic model that they use to this day. The model worked so well for Mart and his family that he wanted to disseminate this information to other health professionals, knowing firsthand that this information was not taught in dental school. As a result, Tim and Mart formed a partnership in 2004 and started Macro Wealth Management.

Mart is also president of Macro Wealth Management, a registered investment advisor (RIA), and registered in multiple states in the financial fields of securities, life and disability insurance, and annuities.

Mart lives in Lake Forest, Illinois, with his wife, Lindsey. They have two children, Riese and Flynn, and a big dog named Bruno.